Happy Children Play

How to Develop a Child's Mental Health and Well-Being

Heather Welch

About the Author

Heather Welch is a Parent, Play Advocate, Educator, and Marketer, who has completed a Masters in Business & Technology & Bachelor's in Education. Also studied play therapy, autism in children, mental health and well being in early years children. She has lived and worked all around the world (Australia, Singapore, and UAE) and is now based in the UK. She has two boys who love to play, so she has learned as much from them as from her teaching experience.

Currently, she is developing an educational brand and sustainable future strategy for Edx Education as well as its educational toys, resources and campaigns to spark children's imagination and creativity. She has written many 'learning through play' articles and has given talks on the subject around the world.

Heather hosts the podcast series which discusses play and learning for all children called Play, Learn & Create.

At the time of writing this book, Heather is also a Play Ambassador for The Genius of Play and a Trustee of a UK charity, *Gecko on the Move*, which provides educational opportunities to children around the world.

As Heather says, let's make the world more playful with happy, healthy children!

Illustrator of the front cover is Helen Weston

A CIP catalogue record for this title is available from the British Library.

Paperback ISBN -- 978-1-915730-31-2
eBook ISBN -- 978-1-915730-32-9

This book is dedicated to all parents and caregivers who want to create a more playful environment to develop children's mental health and well-being.

Table of Contents

Page no:

Introduction

I'm new in the world, and the world is new to me. I come from a place in which all my needs were satisfied. Back then, not so long ago, I was never hungry, thirsty, or cold. But then, I was born, and now I have to adjust to so many new sensations. During these first years of my life, I have so much learning to do!

Luckily, I have a strong resource that will help me learn without even realising it. It will allow me to discover my body and my emotions as well as some basic facts about reality, and it will help me engage with others: first, my parents and caregivers; later, other children like me. That's right! I mean *play*!

As any healthy child, I have loved to play ever since I was a baby and I discovered my hands. Putting a finger inside my mouth helped me discover its shape, size, and flavour, - while also providing me with self-awareness. So every time you see a baby sucking on their thumb, or opening and closing their little hands in front of their eyes, you should know that they are beginning to play.

As I grow up and become a more independent baby, then a toddler, and later a pre-schooler, my games gain in complexity. Besides, I will spend most of my time awake and engaged in playing, and you should know how much it means to me! Playing is not only joyful and entertaining; it also gives us children a sense of purpose and fulfilment, so it is by far the most important activity we do for many years.

And speaking about education, I know that you who are reading this care a lot about how much and how well we learn and we do at school, at home and in life. But let me tell you right from the start that whenever we play, we are learning the most important skills without even realising it! If our parents offer us plenty of opportunities to play, if our caregivers and our teachers at school or kindergarten include play as part of our everyday activities, we'll find it easier to learn how to read, write, count, and understand natural concepts. But most importantly: We'll gain confidence in our abilities, which will make every learning process faster and more effective. Nothing helps me learn more than having a healthy self-esteem.

I can play by myself and, given the right elements appropriate for my current age, and a stimulating environment, I'll soon engage in all sorts of playing activities. You don't need to show me how to play: You need to provide me with plenty of opportunities, and be there for me, watching me with loving eyes, as I play—and grow up healthy and happy!

Chapter 1

Why Play is Important in the Early Years

Where do we begin when we talk about the benefits of play for everyone especially children in their early years?

Play is the way children learn about the world and themselves. While play to the untrained adult's eye can look meaningless, there is a lot more going on than you can see. When children are playing, they are engaged, their imagination is sparked, and they are developing key skills.

Play is so important that adults from all over the world got together and decided to make it clear that play is one of children's rights: "Every child has the right to rest, relax, play and to take part in cultural and creative activities" (UNICEF, 2019). Along with receiving an identity, protection, food, shelter, and education, they should have plenty of time to play.

What is play, what do we mean by *play*? It is an activity in which people (not only children, of course!) take part for enjoyment. As such, playing is voluntary—not mandatory—and spontaneous. It can be free or guided, and it can be solitary or social.

In this chapter, we'll explore the many benefits play has for children, especially in their early years,. Children acquire most of their skills through play: from learning to recognize their own body to acquiring gross, fine motor skills and reaching new milestones; from facing challenges and dealing with frustration to earning persistence, resilience becoming happy and self-confident with every achievement; from recognising basic principles such as cause and effect to acquiring a language, of course, recognising the existence of others around them, and little by little learning social skills. Later, play helps children to better understand and communicate their emotions, solve problems, and develop their creativity.

Of course, play is not the same at every stage of your child's life. Let's consider the benefits and importance of this activity in the first five years and the best toys and elements we can provide for each age.

Playing Baby

A baby's brain develops through play. When they are born, babies have immature brains that will continue to mature thanks to the external surroundings: "Research shows that 75 percent of brain development occurs after birth. Play helps with that development by stimulating the brain through the formation of connections between nerve cells" (Anderson-McNamee and Bailey, 2010).

A baby's growth is directly linked to their playing activities: "An environment enriched with play, sensory play, and play toys provide the perfect life experiences as building blocks.

Lack of play will cause the neuron connections related to play to be lost" (Li, 2022)

Play is needed for the healthy development of your child, particularly when it comes to fine and gross motor skills. Fine motor skills are actions such as being able to hold a spoon or a pencil. Gross motor skills are actions such as walking or climbing.

Newborn to Six Months

Does a newborn baby already play? Some people would doubt it, while others may say that babies can begin playing even before they are born! Ask, for example, Morgan and Richele Rapp. When they found out they were expecting their first son, Jesse, they decided to start bonding right away (WebMD, 2000):

> Sometimes the couple would play games. They'd gently poke first one side of Richele's abdomen, then the other, and watch as Jesse followed their touch by poking the same side back. They even teased him by poking the same side twice and laughed as he poked the "wrong" side back.

After Jesse was born, the couple was thrilled to discover the newborn baby recognized their parents' voices right away, and this helped him calm down easily. The Rapps were right! "Thanks to ultrasound and other high-tech tools allowing a peek inside the womb, scientists have discovered a virtual sensory playground in which your baby is living" (WebMD, 2000). Although there is little to no proof of how much a baby remembers what they have learned in the uterus, playing takes massive importance from the moment your baby is born, and has to face the challenges of the outside world.

Your newborn baby plays by interacting with you. Singing to them, chatting to them, describing what you are doing, nose-poking, smiling, soft-tickling, they all help them to focus on you and create a loving bond. "New babies are drawn to look at the human face and they begin to learn how to 'read' the face of their mother or another caregiver. They carefully watch her eyes and mouth" (Early Years Matters, 2021). When your baby makes any sound, try responding to them. You can also offer your newborn baby different textures for them to explore (even though they won't be able to properly hold them in their hands yet.) Paediatricians recommend giving newborns some "tummy time" every day, when they are awake and active, to help them gain muscular strength and prevent flat heads. Place them on a soft rug or materials that rustle making noise let them feel the texture. Talk to your baby whilst making the transition as not all love being on their tummy. However it is very good for their development.

By the time they enter their second trimester, your baby is no longer a newborn. By this time, they usually have some sort of routine established, they are taking three daily naps but are also awake for longer periods, and playtime is an exciting time in their day. During these months, they usually acquire new mobility, such as learning to hold their heads up, rolling, picking up objects and taking them to their mouth, and even imitating some of your sounds.

Babies learn to roll motivated by their urge to expand their reach, so leaving them on a firm surface on the floor with plenty of safe toys at their reach will motivate them to explore the possibilities their body and their gained muscular strength offer. Offer the baby as many different textures as possible to allow them to discover new materials, such as those used in floor mats and baby gyms.

This age is perfect for introducing rattles. There are some great ones the baby can hold with their hands, but foot rattles are perfect for young babies who still haven't learned to control their hands. They will motivate them to kick and shake their legs and thus help them gain strength. By shaking and making a rattle produce sound, your baby learns about cause and effect, while also having fun You will hear them giggling and even laughing out loud. Join in their fun by rattling with them.

At this age babies explore the world with their mouths, they also might be teething. So teething toys are perfect for giving them the chance to soothe with new textures. Whilst providing some pain relief as their gums are hurting. Please note that some babies grow their first tooth much later, so don't worry if yours still hasn't arrived at this stage. . .

Their developing sense of sight also allows your baby to enjoy gazing at mirrors, even though they won't recognize their image until they are toddlers. Some toys, such as baby gyms, cubes, or activity sets, include small mirrors or even stand with your baby in front of the mirror show talk about what you see and they gaze at the reflections.

By the time your baby turns six months, they are usually able to sit by themselves. As they gain more freedom to move their hands, they will explore more possibilities objects offer to them, such as banging two blocks together or uncovering a toy under a sheet. At this age, they also display an increased interest in books. Sarah Bradley, from *Very Well Family*, suggests providing them with cloth books: "for this age in particular, cloth books are durable, washable, and hold up to a lot of teething-induced chewing" (Bradley, 2021).

Seven to Twelve Months

This is a crucial stage in your baby's development. From seven to nine months is when they reach important milestones, such as learning to sit by themselves and learning to crawl; some can even pull themselves up on furniture. and a few babies are even rehearsing their first steps! You must allow your baby to explore all these new possibilities, giving them plenty of opportunities to practice their new skills.

All this new independence can come with a side of separation anxiety: Babies get more clingy and demanding, refuse to go with strangers (or even with their usual caregivers other than their parents), cry whenever they are left alone, and most of them experience some sort of sleep regression. They are now aware that their parents is not an extension of themselves but a separate person, and therefore, they can leave them! But will they ever come back? If so, when? That's why they cry in anguish even if she has only left the room for a moment!

Through play, babies can overcome this normal part of their development with fewer tears. Playing peek-a-boo or "hide-and-seek" allows them to understand the concept of *object permanence*: They realise that just because they can't see something, it doesn't mean it has ceased to exist. Parents or caregivers leaves but promises to come back right away and they do, which brings reassurance to the baby. This is an important process to go through with your baby to make them feel secure when you are leaving them. Sneaking off can create anxiety which is unnecessary.

This is a great moment for introducing comfort objects, security blankets, or *loveys*, that babies can carry around everywhere and that provide comfort, especially at night time. There are beautiful toys available on the market for babies. However, you don't need to spend a great deal of money, a small piece of cloth or even a piece of old clothing from the main caregiver could be just as effective. Not every baby attaches to a traditional toy but instead finds comfort in ordinary things such as toothbrushes, a spoon, a sippy cup, or a washcloth. As long as the object is safe for the baby and easily washable, that's just fine!

Once your baby acquires mobility, offering them pull toys will motivate them to keep practising their newly discovered abilities. They also enjoy playing chase following the object or toy to try and catch up and you'll discover how much fun they have because of their giggles and laughter. Sure, this time can be challenging for parents and caregivers because you have to get things done around the house, work or with your other children, and your baby won't stay in the same place. Keep safe by using a playpen but remember to allow them plenty of opportunities for free play and exploration whilst safe and entertained.

The average baby starts to walk around their first birthday, or shortly after. However, it isn't a race all babies (and children) develop differently depending on their environment, genetics, abilities, and general well-being. Please don't be worried if they haven't -acquired all the key developmental skills by the exact age mentioned in baby charts. If you are worried, please see a health professional. My own two children developed differently: One was more talkative, and the other was more physical. In any case, as they have grown up, both are talkative and healthy children with different personalities and interests.

Toddler

Once babies start walking, they are considered toddlers (which literally means *the ones who toddle*, that is, that take uneven steps). Toddlers are energetic and have more autonomy than a baby because they can move quite fast, but they still depend a lot on their caregivers for risk aversion. Play helps them improve their motor, language, and social skills, but most importantly its is an essential tool for recognizing and managing their emotions. At this age my children were fun and exhausting as they loved to move , but didn't quite understand the risks. It was always great fun to be with a toddler however challenging as well. Most parents will feel frustrated with having a toddler.

12 to 24 Months

Your toddler is fascinated by their ability to walk and wants to do it all the time. Push toys, ride-on toys, and activity walkers are a great hit at this age. At home they will love building dens from pillows, cushions or cardboard fortresses. This is also a great age for handling musical instruments, but don't spend a lot of money on real ones because your toddler will *not* be careful.

Also, toddlers love to play outdoors. Give them balls, a bucket, big blocks, water or sand trays, toy gardening tools, big wooden blocks. At the same time, let them explore the natural world. They will love to copy whatever you are doing give them a small wheel barrow or gardening tools (safe for toddlers) are a fun idea. They want to touch the leaves and the flowers, to feel the grass barefoot, to pick up stones or shells; just make sure they don't put anything in their mouth!

Their second year is a great time for stimulating their language skills. At this age, toddlers usually say a couple of words but don't talk in full sentences. But they *do* understand a lot! They can point at the words in a book, they can understand and follow simple instructions, and if you narrate your actions while playing with them, helping them understand the world. Reading short simple stories that hold their attention is great for helping their language develop.

People often talk about the "terrible twos" at this age toddlers begin displaying resistance and throwing tantrums. This is actually just your toddler's way of expressing their emotions when they lack the ability to communicate their needs and feelings. Some children do this more than others and you can start to notice their personalities emerging. One of my children was fiercely independent at this age and wouldn't sit in a car seat for anything. However, we start a car seat song and would sing whilst placing him in the car seat.

You can anticipate such negative behaviour and include toys and games in those specific moments of their routines they resist the most: For example, if your toddler refuses to sit in the car seat, keep a special toy for car travel. You can also offer them special toys for their bath time, or their bedtime routines. Try to use a similar routine for e.g playing calmly after dinner, then playing in a warm bath, reading and bedtime. Slowly easing your child into bed.

24 to 36 Months

Two-year-olds display an increased fine motor ability, so by the time your child gets to their second birthday, they will enjoy art, games (make sure the materials are always safe, since some children this age still put things in their mouths). Your task is to provide them with a safe environment to create and express themselves. Try not to worry about making a mess lay a huge mat out and paint on the floor. If the weather is nice go outside and paint on the grass or use chalk on the pavement instead. Some children love to use their hands rather than brushes handprints can make great cards when you cut them out. The results are far less important than the process: they may not be able to draw anything recognisable also they will definitely mix all the colours up whilst painting. However, it's all part of the playing and learning process for children.

Children at this age enjoy simple puzzles as their hand and eye coordination grows. Follow your child's interests some will be more into puzzles others in to construction or messy play. Both my children loved messy play at this age we use to play with sand and water a lot as they loved the tactile feel using their senses. By playing with them, your child learns to pay attention to shape, size, and colours, as well as to cope with negative feelings if they can't assemble them on their first try. However, make sure the puzzles are age-appropriate, not only because of safety reasons (small pieces are a choking hazard) but also because you want them to gain confidence. A puzzle with too many pieces that they can only build with your help will interfere with their individual play and may cause frustration.

At this age, toddlers also spend more time than before engaged in pretend play: Giving them toys such as kitchen sets, toy food, tools, dolls, and costumes, will get them engaged in recreating, and ultimately help them to better understand, all kinds of real-life situations—for example, shopping, going to the doctor, or toilet-training. Pretend play has huge importance for understanding and managing their emotions: "In a New Zealand study, psychologists examined how children handled negative events during pretend plays. They found that children who had more pretend plays with their caregivers were better at regulating their emotions to continue playing" (Li, 2022).

Pre-schooler

It doesn't matter if they are put in childcare or looked after by a stay-at-home parent. By this time in their lives, children spend most of their awake time playing. Generally, they no longer need such long naps (although most pre-schoolers still benefit from one nap after lunch), and they will occupy themselves with long sessions of play.

Three-Year-Old

If you have children at this age you will be experiencing a curious mind, active, talkative, and can be very social. All children are different; for example, my youngest liked his own space at this age it wasn't until he was 4-5 years old that he enjoyed being more social. Although children enjoy the company of other children, at first, they engage in parallel play (more on this in the next chapter), which means they play close to one another, but not necessarily with each other. Once they start realising that other children play like them, they will begin interacting more and more.

They can learn basic social skills, such as taking turns, but don't expect them to share or take turns with their toys easily: When organising a playdate, you can anticipate conflict by bringing extra toys (two cars, two dolls, or two puzzles), or suggesting your child leave their favourite toy at home if you know they will struggle lending it to their friend. Children might relate more to the concept of taking turns rather than sharing. This is easier for young children to understand. Before the playdate ask your child if there is anything they don't want to share, if yes, put it away during the playdate.

At this age, children are also very imaginative. This correlates with their fears, which become more vivid. Playing can help them cope with night terrors or bad dreams. Has your three-year-old got an imaginary friend? They are not the only ones. This is something common and positive: "Imagination fuels creativity and some studies have also found that creative adolescents tend to have had imaginary friends in childhood" (Li, 2022). By "playing" with their imaginary friend, your child is expressing their feelings as well as practising their language skills. Children love to pretend to be animals this is a great way to expand their imagination and be creative.

The gross motor skills of children this age allow them to ride a balance bike, climb up a slide ladder, kick a ball aiming at the goal, run like the wind, or walk on tiptoes! At the same time, by the time they are three, some children already understand the consequences of their actions and can avoid dangerous situations. This doesn't mean you can trust their judgement or let them play without supervision, but at least you don't have to chase them around constantly as you did when they were toddlers. This is a great time for visiting the local playground and letting them burn off their energy and getting fresh air.

Four and Five-Year-Old

As your child grows up, play becomes more complex. Children in preschool still enjoy sensory play, but now they also engage in complex representations and rule-based games with their peers, games in which they have to verbally negotiate. They follow directions from their teachers, and their drawings become rich and imaginative - filled with more details, such as body parts or clothing. Children this age are attracted to letters and numbers, and some can begin to spell their names. They can tell reality from fantasy; they display interest in their surroundings, as well as in other people's feelings and emotions, and they ask a lot of questions.

They still need a lot of messy play and active play, so always encourage them to go outside. By this age, some can ride a bicycle or a scooter without help. Others have learnt to skip or climb a tree. Children take risks at times as parents we want to minimise this think about the language you use to your child e.g instead of using please be careful you can say 'look out for the edge' 'Do you have a plan to climb down the tree?' If the parent shows concern that they may hurt themselves, children will grow insecure about their abilities, so try and trust them and wait before displaying your fear.

To sum up, play is crucial and offers all kinds of benefits for children during their first five years. The most important function of play is helping children find meaning in a world ever increasingly unpredictable, especially since the pandemic (Early Childhood Education in Ethiopia, 2022):

> Children are often left to wonder why their surroundings have failed to protect them. Through play, children can find places for experiences they may have a hard time fully comprehending. When children play, their imagination safely explores areas that may be difficult to talk about.

In the following chapter, we'll explore a few theories about the stages of play as well as their consequences.

Chapter 2

Stages of Play

As we have seen, babies start playing even before they are born. Over the first five years, the ways children engage in play, their purpose, and the complexity of their play change dramatically.

During the 20th century, psychologists studied the different stages of play. In this chapter, we will explore two of the most important theories of play that of Mildred Parten and Jean Piaget about play. Their theories have had a huge influence on education in the Western world.

By learning about these theories and their relevance, we can gain new tools for understanding our child and their current way of playing. It will also help to understand the way your child is playing.

Who Was Mildred Parten?

Mildred Bernice Parten Newhall (1902–1970) was a sociology professor and a researcher at the University of Minnesota's Institute of Child Development. In 1929, while she was working on her doctoral dissertation, she spent several months observing groups of children, aged two to five, while they were playing. "Parten collected data by systematically sampling the children's behaviour. She observed them for pre-arranged 1 minute periods which were varied systematically" (Dean, 2021b) She documented their behaviour and, through extensive observation, she found that social participation in *free play* increased with age, in that children would play without being guided by rules

She first published her dissertation under the title *An Analysis of Social Participation, Leadership, and other Factors in Preschool Play Groups*, and later, in 1932, her classic study on the progressive stages of play appeared in the *Journal of Abnormal and Social Psychology*. Ever since, most behaviour psychologists follow her theory of the six stages of play.

The Six Stages of Play

The first thing Mildred Parten noticed was that, while the first four stages are solitary, the fifth and the sixth show the children cooperating and playing together. As children grow, they don't completely drop off the previous stages but spend more time in the progressive ones. We also notice that the stages do not depend solely on the child's age, but on their current development as well. All child development the stages do not depend solely on the child's age but on their personality and current development. Some children may spend more time in one stage than others. Not to worry, children will go through the stages at their own pace.

Unoccupied Play

This first stage may not seem like play to the inattentive eye, because the child stays rather still and doesn't look like they are playing. However, they are focusing their attention on an object, a situation, or a specific material. Think about a baby manipulating a piece of rag, or chewing on a teething toy. "This is the stage of development where babies or young children seemingly make a lot of random movements with their arms, legs, hands, and feet, but they do not engage with others" (Li, 2022).

Unlike other stages of play, it lacks organisation and planning, so the play seems scattered. However, unoccupied play is important because it is the foundation for the other five stages. "This stage allows children to practise manipulating materials, mastering their self-control and learning about how the world works" (Rymanowicz, 2015). By engaging in unoccupied play, children learn about the qualities of their surroundings, understand facts such as gravity, weight, texture, or sound, and develop their patience. A hungry baby may get distracted playing with their spoon, allowing their caregiver enough time to finish setting up their meal.

Although this form of play gets less frequent as the child advances in their development, you can now and then notice it in older children: A boy that seems distracted looking through the car window may actually be engaged in staring at the raindrops on the glass, telling himself all kinds of stories, and playing in a certain way.

Solitary Play

During the second stage, also known as independent play, children engage in any kind of activity, without interacting with others, but fully committed to their play. Toddlers often enjoy spending time with their shape-sorters or bead mazes, piling up blocks, or pressing the buttons on their talking puppy over and over again. Pre-schoolers can create fabulous little worlds of their own with their dolls, their stuffed animals, or their cars. Once children have developed language, we can often hear them talking to themselves during solitary play.

While some parents show concern when children play on their own for too long, this is a normal stage that also allows them to learn while enjoying themselves. “When children engage in solitary play, they are able to explore freely, master new personal skills like new motor or cognitive skills, and prepare themselves to play with others” (Rymanowicz, 2015).

Although solitary play is more common in toddlers aged two or three, the amount of time a child spends engaged in this sort of play also depends on their personality. Thus, extroverted children might jump to the following stage faster, while introverted children play by themselves for longer. Also, an only child may engage in independent play more than children who grow up with one or more siblings.

Onlooker Play

In this stage, also known as spectator play, the child becomes aware of other children playing but does not join them. They sometimes talk to them, without, however, taking an active part in the game. This doesn't mean they are lonely or shy; it's just another normal stage of social learning. "This is the first sign of children showing interest in social aspects of play by observing, asking questions, and making suggestions to others" (Li, 2022).

By observing how other children play, a child learns social rules and relationships. Think of a three-year-old who isn't still ready to play hide-and-seek in the park with their older brother, but still pays a lot of attention to what's going on.

Parallel Play

In this fourth stage, children are playing close to each other, but not *with* each other. They may even use the same of toys, look at the other child and copy some of their actions, but they don't interact with the other child, or the interaction is minimal and has no significance for the play. "Even though there is no direct social interaction between the child and other children, there is a social element in the fact that they choose to play with the same toys" (Li, 2022). Because they still lack the social ability to share, during parallel play it is important that children are given enough toys or elements for each of them to engage in the activity on their own. Kindergarten teachers know this!

During this stage, when we usually set the first playdates for our toddlers, we notice that as the children sit close to one another, each one picks up a toy, and little by little, the nearby peers will become more interesting than the toys. For many, then, this stage is a "warm-up" for the following, more social stages of play (Rymanowicz, 2015).

Associative Play

By the time a pre-schooler turns four years old, they usually become more interested in being with other children and sharing the play with them. "Associative play allows children to begin practising what they have observed through onlooker and parallel play. They can start to use their newfound social skills to engage with other children or adults during an activity or exploration" (Rymanowicz, 2015).

Even though they are still focused on their interests and don't share a common goal, they choose to play with the same toys or elements and usually exchange opinions or comments on each other's play. Their activities are loosely connected, although the children don't attempt to change the way the other children are playing.

"As children grow older, associative play becomes more common. This stage of play teaches children how to get along with others. It teaches cooperation and improves language skills" (Li, 2022). Imagine two children dressing up their dolls and talking about what each other is going to put on next. Or imagine a group of children splashing each other in the pool, laughing, sometimes splashing all at the same time, and sometimes doing it alone.

Cooperative Play

In the sixth and final stage, social interaction becomes more complex, as children are brought together by a common goal: They can decide upon roles for playing house, playing a board game following stated rules, or joining forces to build a huge castle with their matching construction sets or linking cubes. This stage usually occurs by the time the children are five years old and have acquired enough verbal skills to express their ideas and understand others as well. Although children as young as three can take part in cooperative play, young children tend not to take part because they don't have the same ability to express themselves through words (Li, 2022).

Cooperative play usually creates opportunities for children to fit into a specific role among their peers: "There is a distinct sense of belonging or not belonging among the children in the group. Only one or two children direct the goal-oriented group activities. The children may divide labor according to their roles" (Li, 2022).

Something normal for this stage is that children argue and get into conflict as they try to figure out ways in which to negotiate and cooperate. "It is sometimes difficult for young children to share, take turns and negotiate control in these types of play scenarios" (Rymanowicz, 2015). In any case, cooperative play offers them plenty of opportunities to express their emotions, recognize other children's feelings, and improve their problem-solving abilities.

Although Parten's theory is widely accepted, it has received criticism. As Dean (2021b) mentions, not every child necessarily follows the types of play as a sequence. Also, independent play is not a sign of immaturity, in the same way that some toddlers being occasionally able to cooperate doesn't mean they are above their age. Finally, interaction among children is dependent not only on their personality and maturity, but also on the familiarity among groups of children: Toddlers playing together with their siblings may cooperate, while older kids may opt for independent play if they find themselves surrounded by unfamiliar children, no matter if they are the same age.

Comparison With Piaget's Theory

Jean Piaget, a Swiss psychologist changed the way we understand children and their development. By constantly creating and recreating his own model of reality. Piaget saw the child achieving mental growth, simply by integrating simpler concepts into higher – level concepts at each stage. According to Piaget, there are four stages of cognitive development (Dean, 2021a), which are:

Sensorimotor stage, in which babies and toddlers depend on their five senses to know the world and are fascinated by newly discovered sensations.

Pre-operational stage, in which children already have some ideas about the world, they can represent them and put them into words, but they can't make any logical connections.

Concrete operational stage, in which children improve at problem-solving and can deduct logical operations in concrete terms.

Formal operational stage, in which children start thinking and conceiving the world as adults.

Piaget also categorised play into types according to the child's behaviour: practice play, symbolic play, and play-with-rules (Albrecht, 2016). While babies and young toddlers engage more often in practice play, which consists of repetitions of specific actions, older toddlers and pre-schoolers opt for symbolic play (role-playing, wearing costumes, recreating everyday scenes, etc.). Older children who are, as per Parten's definitions, already at the collaborative play stage, prefer play-with-rules, which demands negotiating and accepting common ground.

Piaget was the first to compare play for children to work for adults, meaning that play—although by definition pleasurable and self-rewarding—is a serious cognitive task.

He also addressed play and its stages. Like Mildred Parten, he based his work on direct observations of children playing, starting with his daughter. But unlike Parten, who emphasised the social aspects of play, Piaget understood types of play in terms of how they help the child's brain development.

Another difference is the age at which changes occur. Piaget set the pre-operational stage until the child turns seven years old, while Parten acknowledged children aged four or five are already involved in cooperative play, including rules. We have all seen pre-schoolers learning simple board games, or following directions, so I think any parent or educator in the 21st century could say that Piaget's age divisions are at least inaccurate. However, he laid the groundwork for further studies, and he was among the first academics to recognise that children think and look at the world differently than adults. And without his theory, we wouldn't be aware of most of what we know today about the importance of play for children.

What Can We Do?

If we consider Parten's theory and the six stages of play she proposed, how can parents/educators further stimulate their child's development? First of all, no matter how old our child is, the most important gift we can grant them is *free time.* Healthy children will play when given enough opportunities, even if they lack other resources, such as toys. Sadly, in today's world, most children are dragged from activity to activity, and hardly find the time to engage in free play.

This is because "The amount of time children spend in uninterrupted self-directed play–when no one is teaching them, when they are free to decide what and how to play–has declined tremendously in educational settings and in the home lives" (Albrecht, 2016).

It's common for children to spend a lot of their time awake at school or nursery, and not every school curriculum includes enough free play. Breaktimes are scarce, children are rushing from one extra-curricular activity to another, and by the time they get home, they still have to study, practise a sport or a musical instrument, learn a second or third language, or do homework. Screens directly absorb them from a tender age, and because many children live in cities, not all of them have enough outdoor play:

When it comes to babies during unoccupied play, we simply have to let them explore their surroundings and discover the possibilities their body offers them. Placing a baby on a safe surface, leaving within their reach a few age-appropriate toys, and allowing them to move freely are the best ways we can encourage this first stage. Babies also need plenty of reassurance, physical touch, constant displays of affection, and enough time to sleep. However, this is not the time to "teach" them how to play: We can play with them, but they'll figure it out by themselves when all of their basic needs are met.

Solitary play may worry some parents, who feel the need to intervene and "rescue" their child that seems lonely. But, as we have seen, it is also a normal stage that helps children entertain themselves. It offers them the chance to improve their concentration, and it also keeps them occupied when we are busy with household chores or the home office. Some toddlers can't play by themselves and are constantly craving adult attention.

Providing your child some minutes of meaningful connection (sitting at their level, simply watching them play, not leading them, and engaging by asking questions) may motivate them to play on. It's important that during those times you put your mobile phone down and truly focus on your child. Pay attention to what they have to say, and once they feel comfortable enough, you'll both discover they don't *need* you to play all the time with them.

You can also invite toddlers to play with a new toy by using it yourself, as Albrecht (2016) suggests:

> The best source of play cues is you. When you pick up a toy and play with it or sit down at the table to see if you can fit a puzzle piece into the puzzle, the

toy or puzzle becomes very interesting to toddlers. This strategy for inviting play is an excellent way to interest toddlers in new materials or props.

As toddlers and pre-schoolers advance to other stages of play, our role is to provide them emotional support, as well as tools for understanding and communicating their emotions. "When toddlers play, they subtly adjust the way they play to the play of their friends to keep the play going–an early indicator that they understand how others are feeling" (Albretch, 2016).

Putting into words their feelings, as well as helping them identify another child's emotions, will help them become empathetic and move forward to parallel play and cooperative play. They will still need your help for solving conflicts with their peers as well as for dealing with frustration, but by the time they are playing with their peers, the best you can do is to stay close and wait before intervening. That will give them the chance to try and solve problems on their behalf.

By understanding the importance play has for our child's well-being, and cognitive, physical, emotional, and social development, we can make the best efforts to provide them with plenty of opportunities to choose their play during the day. Every parent wants the best for their children, and we may believe that providing them with all of the extracurricular activities we can squeeze into our already too-busy schedule.

But playing freely—without being constantly guided by an adult and without strict timeframes—gives children the chance to learn more while also enjoying themselves. Free play develops creativity, problem solving, self-confidence, leadership, communication and language.

Your child doesn't need you to play with them constantly, but they *do* enjoy sharing some of their play with you! In the following chapter, we'll take a closer look at how we can play with our children and the ways it strengthens our loving bond.

Chapter 3

Let's Play and Learn Together

When was the last time you sat with your child and played with them? Do you think you spend enough time playing with your child?

No matter what you respond, if we asked the child, the answer would probably be "I want them to play *more*!" And this is not meant to blame you, of course! Given our current busy schedules that include work, school activities, household chores, and family commitments, we have little time on our hands. Whether you run your business, work at an office, or are a stay-at-home parent, you have to juggle a lot of responsibilities.

Play is wonderful if you can let yourself go and become involved in your child's play. When speaking to friends they find it difficult if their children don't follow the rules when playing. They love structure in their play, however you will find that free play is at times chaotic, and unstructured as we are entering our child's mind and having a taste of how they want to express themselves.

Although we may be well aware of how important play is for our children, many times we treat it as something that can wait. That's okay, and your children can understand it, as long as you don't keep them waiting forever! It is important to take time out to spend with your child each day and to let them know when you will be able to be with them. So, giving your children the knowledge that this is a ten-minute playtime will help to set an expectation

Your child can—and will—play without you. They need many daily hours of free play to gain all the benefits of this activity. Instead of thinking of playtime as another task in their busy schedule, you should provide them with several opportunities for play throughout the day. Further on, we'll provide you with some suggestions to encourage independent play. But in this chapter, we will approach the benefits both adults and children alike gain when they dedicate some part of their day to playing together.

That's right: Playing with your child is not only necessary for them, but it's also great for you! "Playing with children builds lasting bonds. Playing allows parents to appreciate the uniqueness of each child. Playing with children can also be a stress reducer for overworked parents. Laughing and relaxing are important to your own well-being" (Anderson-McNamee and Bailey, 2010).

One final note: The advantages of playing with children don't apply only to parents, but to any caregiver as well, and of course, also to educators.

Our Role to Make Play Relevant

Play is a natural activity that babies are doing from before they are born, it is not our role as parents to teach a child *how* to play. Our job is to give them as many opportunities as possible, to help them apply their learning to real-life situations, and to be emotionally available for them. "You are your child's first teacher and much of that teaching happens through play. Play helps your child learn the rules of your family and what is expected of him or her. As children grow, play helps them learn how to act in society" (Anderson-McNamee and Bailey, 2010).

How can we motivate them to get them to play more? One of the most important things is to follow their lead whether it be cars, books, blocks, colours, shapes, the garden or dinosaurs. You may want your child to learn shapes or numbers, but you can't force them to be interested in them just because "they need to learn." Remember that playing has to be self-rewarding and free! Before introducing new toys or games that you consider age-appropriate, check whatever toys, games, or activities they already like what are they usually draw to. To recognize those kinds of things, you have to spend time with your toddler or child: Listen to them, ask them questions, and let them know you are interested as well.

This doesn't mean you can't introduce them to new interests—of course, you can, and if you are an educator, it is your job. Just make sure you don't push them, but rather spark their natural curiosity and imagination. By exploring and experimenting, children learn without realising. At home, you can introduce open-ended toys such as construction blocks in different shapes and sizes, or multi-coloured pebble stones to encourage design thinking and solving problems.

We can use our playtime to teach our children how to think. In a previous work of mine I propose five ways that can be easily applied to play:

Give choices. Allow your child to pick the colour of the toy, creative design, or what game to play. Encourage them to give reasons for their choice.

Listen. Be there when they are pretend playing. Listen to what they are saying. Ask them questions to make them explain the different concepts.

Explore. Play is a great opportunity for children to explore taking chances and controlled risks. Take a step back and let your children climb a tree, prepare a magic potion (with safe elements), or let them change the rules of one of their favourite games.

Experiment. Encourage them to try new things! Maybe they always want to wear the same princess costume. What if today they play to be firefighters instead?

Embrace experiences or opportunities. Go out of your comfort zone! Try going to a different playground, or arranging a playdate with a classmate they don't know so well.

Styles of Parenting

Some parents find it easy to enjoy playing with their children, while others struggle. Much of it depends on your parenting style. In the 1960s developmental psychologist Diana Baumrind put forth four parenting styles that most psychologists accept today. "In recent years, however, parenting experts have coined a number of unofficial (and commonly debated) styles" (Brody, 2021).

This is a funny question we probably all think about and not necessarily discuss "what style of parent are you?" Have you ever thought of this? If I think about our parenting my husband would be authoritative with a touch of helicopter and natural. When I asked him he said my parenting style was a melting pot of attached, natural and tiger.

The classification below is meant only as a guide, as most of us don't fall 100% of the time, but it may help to recognize some of your tendencies. By acknowledging them, you can value your strengths and focus on improving your weaknesses.

Authoritarian Parents

Because they are concerned with their children following the rules, these parents can sometimes display little affection and appear cold towards them. Authoritarian parents can find it challenging to allow messy play or to enjoy free play. On the other hand, spending some quality time with their children may help them loosen up while still keeping their authority.

Authoritative Parents

These parents want their children to follow the rules, not out of fear, but out of understanding the consequences of their decisions. They are open to dialogue, communicative, and caring. This style receives lots of praise! According to Jephtha Tausig, clinical psychologist and clinical supervisor at the Icahn School of Medicine at Mount Sinai

Medical Center (New York), "It's usually what ends up being most comfortable for both children and parents because it tends to reduce conflict" (Brody, 2021). These parents usually feel comfortable playing all kinds of games with their children and embrace every opportunity to help them learn while having fun.

Permissive Parents

They are the opposite of authoritarian. Because they want to become their child's best pals, they allow them to do as they like and set no limits. They say "yes" to most of their children's requests, and that also includes playing with them a lot! "How about turning the table upside down and building a fort?" "Sure! It sounds great!" They don't care if the house is messed up as they value it as part of their children "being children." They can be fun as playtime buddies, but they may find it hard to solve conflict when it arises.

Free-ranged Parents

According to Lenore Skenazy, author of the book *Free-Range Kids*, these parents want more than anything to allow their children independence: They trust them to do many things on their own, such as walking to school or preparing meals. Their children probably engage in independent play, but if you are this kind of parent, remember that just because you get involved in their play doesn't mean you are controlling them.

Helicopter Parents

Unlike the previous style, these parents are all about supervising and protecting their children. They are likely to engage in all sorts of (safe) guided activities. However, your challenge if you are a helicopter parent is allowing some independent play as well and letting them take some risks.

Attached Parents

The term attachment parenting, which was coined by Dr. William Sears and his wife Martha (2001), refers more to raising babies by physically and emotionally addressing their needs. Attachment parents may enjoy a lot of physical touches, such as tickles, picking up the baby, singing to them, etc. Attached parenting needs to remember allow their children for unoccupied play.

Tiger Parents

To make it more inclusive, I've changed the common term "tiger mum" that first appeared in the book *Battle Hymn of the Tiger Mother* by Amy Chua. Similar to authoritarian parents, those who adopt this style expect a lot from their children and are always pushing them to give their best. A tiger parent may love STEM games, chess, or educational apps, and will probably strive to make their child the best. Just remember that playing is supposed to be free and fun! Tiger parents need to remember that play is about being free and there may not be a productive outcome from play.

Natural Parents

These parents care about our natural environment, the impact our food choices have on our health, and the connections between all of our actions and decisions. They love outdoor play and activities and will instil in their children a love for nature and exploration. If you fall under this parenting style, try to be flexible and don't lose your cool if your child prefers to play with mainstream toys now and then.

There is no right or wrong way of parenting. It depends on your family, environment, your own upbringing, education, experiences, culture, and so much more. As we mentioned at the start, most parents don't parent just one way but they may often use many of these styles.

Building Strong Relationship

Playing with your child is one of the best ways to further connect with them and build a loving and long-lasting bond. In the meantime, here are some more strategies you can implement for communicating with and understanding them.

Building your child's self esteem

Every caregiver and parent can do a lot for a child's self esteem. However there are certain factors that need to be present in order for a child to have healthy self esteem.

Sense of security, they need to feel safe and secure about who they are and about their future. A sense of belonging, like most people it is very important for a child to feel accepted and loved by the people around them. This starts with families, and as they grow older extends to family, peers, teachers, and community members. Without this acceptance, a child will not have a group identity and will feel lonely and rejected. A sense of purpose, children need to have set goals, a sense of direction that they want to go in. Sense of personal competence a child needs to feel confident they have the ability to face challenges. Sense of responsibility, need an opportunity to show off their capabilities. Allow them time to be independent. Sense of encouragement, allowing children to be independent is great however they need positive feedback. They want to know how they perform.

As parents and caregivers, we need to build our child confidence. Easy ways to influence your child's self-esteem is to keep up a conversation with them, share interests, tell them you love them, accept them just how they are, spend time with them, encourage friendships, take an interest in their school work and hobbies.

Praise Them

Giving your children praise in the right amount and for the right reasons—such as encouraging effort instead of only praising good results—helps them gain more confidence and boosts their self-esteem. However, for praise to be effective, it should be meaningful and honest. Avoid empty phrases such as "great job!" when they show you their latest toy building. Instead, point out specific reasons leading you to praise them: "I like how you arranged the blocks by colour! How did you come up with such an idea?" Ask them to tell you about their picture and what they like about it?

Practise Active Listening

Whenever your child has something to say, even if it's still baby talk, try to give them your undivided attention. Keep eye contact. You may even sit down or kneel at their level so your eyes meet theirs. Try to repeat what your child said with different words to show them that you understand, or ask them further questions. If they lack the verbal abilities to communicate, they can still point!

Show Them Empathy

If your child is upset, frustrated, sad, or angry, instead of nagging them or telling them "it's no big deal," show them that you can relate to them. Try to put their emotions into words, as this will help them recognize them and handle them in the near future: "You are upset because your building fell down." It's okay to comfort them, but allow them to experience the emotion instead of rushing to find a solution. Instead of solving the problem right away, try to make them an active part of it: "What could we use to make it stronger?"

Engage in Positive Contact

Don't wait for your child to do something particularly amazing to display your affection. Sometimes, just a kind tap on their back, a casual hug, or some kind words can do wonders for your bond, especially if your children are always testing your limits and you find yourself correcting their behaviour, repeating the rules over and over, or making a big effort not to react. When you smile at your child, or when you tell them something nice, it helps you counterbalance the times in which you engage in not-so-positive ways.

Play With Them or Let Them Play?

Play is the natural state of a healthy child but what happens if playing doesn't come naturally to you. Some parents love their children and enjoy spending time with them, whether riding a bicycle, watching movies on television, baking cookies, or going to fun places as a family, but still feel like they don't know how to engage in their play, or they don't enjoy it.

It's no wonder we adults have forgotten how to play. Our culture forces us to give up on leisure: "Many adults have an unhealthy relationship with time. Our collective obsession with productivity, work and self-optimization have left us with this relentless feeling that we are always behind the ball, never getting enough done" (Strauss, 2021).

However, once you manage to disconnect yourself from all these social imperatives, playing with your child helps you to unwind, lowering your stress levels and improving your well-being, while also strengthening the bond with your child.

Playing with a baby is as easy as simply responding to them. Repeating their babble, clapping your hands, and smiling whenever they shake their little feed or do an effort to turn on their back, or giving them everyday items to encourage sensory play might be enough. With your toddler, you can begin by staying close by and watching them play, and later include more elements to their game. If they pick up a doll, you can give her a hat or a pair of sunglasses; if you take them to the park, you can help them develop their gross motor skills by kicking a ball against a tree (it doesn't matter if they don't score!) Including them in everyday activities, such as cooking, sweeping the floor, or watering the plants, can also be a kind of play if you make it fun and silly.

Preschoolers are more into imaginary play, so try engaging in their pretend play, accepting their invitation to buy food at the supermarket they created, or joining their teddy bear tea party. School children already offer you choices such as playing board games or video games, but you can still play physically: doing a bicycle race, skateboarding, playing catch, table tennis, or any other activity they like. And you don't need to let them win! "Kids this age actually thrive on competition, and activities with a lot of sensory input are a great way for kids to focus their energy and then feel very calm and content afterwards" (Mlynek, 2020)

How can you even begin to play with a child if this is something that doesn't come naturally? Vicki Glembocki, a mum of two girls, found herself in the same situation as one-third of British parents who admit they don't know how to play or they find playing with their kids boring (Glembocki, 2012):

> This is embarrassing, but I'll come right out and say it: I had completely forgotten how to play [...] Whenever Blair would ask me to build a fort or say, "Let's play restaurant," my gut reaction was always the same: "Do I have to?"

Some of the strategies she started implementing were to make play a priority in her already busy mum schedule, which meant offering ten minutes a day of uninterrupted play; using the "yes and…" response suggested by Mary Carpenter, a director of an American improvisation comedy; or doing unexpected silly actions to keep the girls surprised (such as wearing a bowl as a hat while cooking dinner).

Eventually, when she got on board with playing with her girls, Vicki discovered they only needed her to engage for a little while before going back to their games, but she's still grateful the exercise reminded her how to play: "It turned out my inner 5-year-old is a lot cooler than I'd remembered. I'm so glad we had the chance to go to a tea party together again" (Glembocki, 2012)

And if after all these ideas, you still realise you are not play-material, you shouldn't feel guilty. Playing with your children should not be about becoming the perfect parent, something done out of guilt, something you do because you can't say no, or because your children can't entertain themselves unless you are involved (Strauss, 2021).

And, in any case, you are not alone! The same happens to Edan Lepucki, a mum of three children under ten, when she realised that forcing herself to play with her toddler (who preferred strong, physical games) was turning her more into an obstacle than anything else: "I said no and stop all day long, and when my scolding seeped into the playing, I felt guilty and frustrated. I was a terrible playmate, a tired mother who did little beyond obstructing" (Lepucki, 2021). In time, she accepted that her gift for her children was stepping out and letting them build their little worlds, as she had done when she was little:

> My parents allowed me private worlds of my own creation, and they respected them. I imagine they felt the same joy I do when I watch my children playing without me; my daughter opens a bakery as her older brother bounces on a giant rubber ball. The baby fills his garbage truck with blocks. Each of us enters his or her own separate sphere. This, I've realized, is my favourite part of mothering. My looking away and then observing.

Being there for children who play by themselves is even more important than handing them the appropriate toys. In the following chapter, we'll give you plenty of tips to encourage independent play.

Chapter 4

Ideas to Motivate Children to Play

It is easy for me to say playing comes naturally for children when given the right motivation. However, what is that motivation and how can we work with our children to be more playful?

Some babies enjoy solitary play as soon as they can sit on their own and hold toys with their hands, while some older children struggle to enjoy their own company and constantly claim their parents' attention. Here we will explain the benefits of independent play, the reasons why some children find it harder than others to achieve, and some ideas to motivate them.

Benefits of Independent Play

Solitary or independent play has plenty of advantages for our children as well as for ourselves because it gives us a much-needed break. First of all, when your child engages in independent play, they learn they don't need others to have fun! Enjoying your own company is crucial for living well in later years. It also lets them explore their imagination and become problem-solvers, something we adults can constrain without realising when we guide them too much during our play together.

Another benefit, further discussed in Chapter 6, is that independent play prepares a child for school: "When you teach them how to be happy in their own company, they'll happily step into the new learning phase without you holding onto them" (Arora, 2022) .

Why Do Children Find It Difficult to Play on Their Own?

It feels like toddlers demand attention from their parents 24/7, and although they may seem clingy, in fact, they are struggling to build a safe attachment. If your child demands your constant attention, it's not because they need you around all the time, but because they are lacking a meaningful connection. Maybe you are near them all the time, but distracted or busy doing chores or using the computer, and what they claim is that special look, that undivided attention they feel they are not getting. We can all be guilty of being distracted especially with multiple children.

Sometimes, it helps simply put aside a few minutes of your daily routine to simply be with your toddler. Show them that you care about them, ask them questions, and provide reassurance. Once your children get used to receiving regular quality time, , this may be all they need to gain independence start to play independently.

When your child becomes clingy, make sure you praise them for whatever independent play they achieve: “Look at you flipping the pages of your book! We can read it together at night time.” This will enhance the desired behaviour. Anticipate them both when you play with them, as well as when your playtime is over: “Okay, as soon as I finish peeling the potatoes, I’ll play with you until the water boils. I had a great time colouring with you. Now, I’ll paint one more flower and then I have to do laundry. You can finish colouring the page and then you show it to me!” Anticipation, as long as you keep your word, will provide them with security.

If your child is okay with you taking an onlooking role and playing on their own, you can slowly remove yourself from their sight, little by little. Start by telling them you are going to wash your hands and then come back straight away. Then, you can leave them for a couple of minutes, always telling them where you are going, and promising you’ll come back (and keeping your promise). Eventually, they’ll realise they can keep playing and you are still available if they need you.

Thus said, if a child still refuses to play, you can’t coax them to do it. They need to have the intrinsic motivation to want to play. Let's look at ideas for independent play next. Play should be free and pleasurable, and if you turn it into an obligation, then it isn't playing at all! Sometimes, the best you can do is tolerate your child staring at you with an accusatory look while you keep doing whatever you need to be doing and accept their boredom as part of the learning process.

Encouraging Independent Play

Your child doesn't need to play with you for a long time. Provided that they get regular quality interactions, they only need your help finding the right motivation. We hear a lot of parenting experts talk about connection before perfection, by which they mean you should simply have a meaningful interaction with your child before trying to make the play perfect. Children will learn more by making small mistakes and having to problem-solve them than by being shown or told the right way. If you provide them with safe, age-appropriate materials, maybe they won't even need your guidance to keep playing independently. Here we'll give you some useful tips.

Sensory Play

We consider sensory play any kind of pleasurable interaction that stimulates the senses of the child: seeing, touching, smelling, hearing, or tasting. In that way, having your toddler help you prepare a salad can be a great sensory experience! It plays a huge role in your child's development "especially if they are still quite young or have additional needs. This type of play helps children to focus their attention, and it can also help them to develop their fine motor skills" (Welch, 2022b). Here are some elements that stimulate independent sensory play, also known as *messy play*.

Sand and water. Whether at the beach or in the playground's sandbox, these are great elements to keep your child busy during those long summer days. "Creating a sand and water play area is a great way to encourage your children to get creative, while also ensuring they stay busy for hours on end" (Welch, 2022b). They provide just the right conditions for experimenting and learning without realising it. Young toddlers acquire basic maths knowledge by measuring, pouring, emptying, and filling. Older children benefit from open-ended activities, such as digging a hole or making a sandcastle. By adding food colouring and soap, you can also provide them with a great rainbow foam.

Playdough and slime. You can buy them or try making them at home. These materials allow all kinds of possibilities, from creating new objects to counting the parts, and mixing the colours. Some children love them, although touching something slimy or sticky can be unpleasant at first for others. If that's the case, you can attempt to handle these materials with objects such as cookie cutters, plastic forks, knives, wooden sticks, or rolling pins.

Different types of materials. Exploring different materials like tin foil or baking paper. Letting them experience the different textures, thicknesses, crunchiness, and scent has a huge impact on sensory awareness. You can use fabric scraps for crafting a fabric book, a play mat, for playing peek-a-boo and teaching them about object permanence as we have already explained, or for creating costumes. You don't need to spend money on fabric. You can empty one of your closet drawers on the bed and let your toddler have a blast! Make a treasure box for children to fill up with these items. When it comes to babies, make sure the materials are safe, non-toxic, and not too small so they can't choke on them.

Other safe materials you can find at home. Wool, cotton balls, flour, rice, dry pasta, buttons, silk flowers, pipe cleaners, cardboard tubes, ice cubes, muffin caps, salt, feathers, grass, leaves, shaving foam–anything can be turned into sensory play material. Just make sure you supervise it. Provide your child with elements to mix, to fill, or tools to work on, and try not to worry too much about the mess while your child is exploring. If you worry about mess, try to prepare a space that is easy to clean afterwards or do it in the garden.

Construction Play

Building sets, bricks, linking cubes, wood blocks, rainbow pebbles, marble mazes, stacking cups or rings offer many possibilities for developing children's imagination as well as improving their fine motor skills. When building something, your toddler learns about science, maths, geometry, art cause and effect, as well as patience, perseverance, and how to deal with frustration.

Open-ended toys, in particular, offer the child plenty of options and variables. "If you are choosing an open-ended toy, the kid would indulge with it for a longer duration without distraction. If there were an option of playing with the same object in different ways, kids would love it" (Arora, 2022). Here are some suggestions, although your child will probably come up with 20 more once they start to explore all of the possibilities these toys offer.

Design. Instead of having the perfect doll house with a lifelike kitchen set that includes a microwave and a dishwasher, hanging curtains made of flowery fabric, and a soft bed, your child can create their dream house from scratch by using construction toys, reused elements such as cardboard boxes, plastic containers, or empty pen cartridges. Open-ended toys have abstract shapes that allow children to make them whatever they want them to be. Their house can be of any size or shape. How about including a slide from the roof to the ground floor? Or adding beds for the doll's pets as well? Anything can happen!

Build the tallest tower. Or the longest car racetrack. Or the weirdest spaceship! Unlike board games, which are more appropriate for older kids, construction games are not about competing against each other, but about breaking the child's own limits. Besides, these toys are perfect for when children enter the cooperative play stage, as they may offer them a common goal and problem-solving situations without making it about "who beats whom".

Design newest car with the linking cubes. Given a set of open-ended toys, two children will create two different toys. Ten children will create ten different toys as well! The same child can arrange and rearrange their designs and therefore, unlike battery-operated, single-purpose expensive toys your child may keep playing with them over and over again without getting tired. If they want to turn the car into a helicopter, a boat, or an plane, all of a sudden they get a new toy!

Rainbow Pebbles vs. traditional stacking toys. There's nothing wrong with an old set of sorting or stacking rings or cups, but Rainbow Pebbles offer more possibilities when it comes to teaching your children about shapes, colours, and fine motor skills. This is because they can arrange them in different ways, sort them for size, shape, or colour, and create an infinite variety of designs. A stacking set of six cups doesn't qualify as an open-ended toy, although it can be great for babies and young toddlers who still lack the ability to manipulate more complex toys.

Role-Play

Role-play is crucial for understanding how the world works. When they play restaurant or set a tea party for their stuffed animals, or they dress up as their favourite movie characters, children are not *pretending*; they are recreating reality as they understand it and playing by their rules! Through role-play, children express their emotions, acquire verbal skills, they learn how to behave in certain situations (or feel it's safe to misbehave this time), it helps them become aware of others and develop their empathy as well as other social skills. Here are some suggestions to encourage independent role-play.

Being the caregiver or parent. Offer them some of your clothes, hats or bags, but if you want to delight your child, allow them to play with real grown-ups' objects, such as a wallet, a purse, or an old mobile phone (be careful with batteries and small parts!), your keys, etc. Try not to laugh when they imitate your tone of voice when setting some boundaries for their dolls and such. They are practising empathy without realising and displaying their understanding of your rules.

Turning into an animal. Cover a coffee table with an old sheet and tell your toddler it's a transformation machine: and as they walk in, they turn into animals. Jumping like frogs, running on their fours like a dog, waving their arms as they fly is a great way for children to move their bodies. This kind of role-play encourages them to pay close attention to nature.

Becoming a prince or princess. This role-play allows them to feel special and boosts their self-esteem and have fun dressing up. Never laugh at your prince or your princess, just tell them how great they look!

Playing superheroes. This is a great role-play for engaging with other children, expressing their fears, and finding the tools to face them, and physically exploring their gross motor skills: running really fast, climbing tall trees, expressing their courage, etc. However, always supervise this play, to make sure they are not taking risks (some toddlers are not aware yet that their cape *doesn't* actually make them fly) or getting into a physical fight.

Playing house. When your child prepares a meal with their pretend food, creates a supermarket, takes their dolls to the doctor, or transforms the armchair into a driver's seat, they are recreating everyday events, learning from these situations, and gaining a better understanding them.

Active Play

Children need regular exercise—as we all do—and they get it through active play: Running, jumping, climbing, digging a hole, picking up seashells, anything goes!

Being active inside and out. Children need plenty of outdoor play to be healthy, happy, and active. However, sometimes we have to stay indoors because of the weather conditions or because we don't have the time to take them to the park. If the pandemic taught us anything about indoor play is that we can be active even in small spaces! I, enjoy building dens, obstacle course and playing floor is lava around the living areas with my children. Your child can build a den with furniture and blankets, an obstacle course with pillows and cushions, or a spider web with a ball of string. You can seize the advantages of technology and engage them in a yoga class for children on YouTube, or a choreography of their favourite song.

Exploring nature. Going outside allows your child to discover the natural world, explore, and "When your child is outside, they probably have more space and freedom for big movements like running, jumping, kicking, and throwing. Physical activities like these are good for your child's fitness and physical development" (Raising Children Network, 2019). Such as enough vitamin D, improving their sight, fresh air can help them sleep better. When they play outside you always have to supervise them, you take a step back and let them play independently create their own games. Climbing a tree is a great way to teach risk, talk to them about being safe and making sure it is stable enough to stand. If you can climb up can you get back down?

Digital Play

If your toddler is constantly exposed to screens, and the only way you can do some stuff around is by turning on the television or handing them a tablet, that may explain why they can't focus their attention on toys and achieve independent play. Screens interfere with children's attention spans, and they provide stimulation, but they don't encourage their imagination.

While the American Academy of Paediatrics (AAP) recommends no screen time at all for babies and toddlers under 18 months, "UK's Chief Medical Officer suggests a 'precautionary approach' balanced against the potential benefits of using screen devices" (National Childbirth Trust, 2019). Even though not every expert agrees on how much time is appropriate, everyone suggests limiting and supervising the time our children spend with devices because prolonged use of screens can affect their sight, it is linked to childhood obesity and poor sleep quality.

It's not all bad news, though. The truth is that technology is part of our everyday lives, and many parents rely on it to have a little time for preparing a meal. Not to mention that the pandemic has taught us how video calls could reduce the distance between loved ones. Even the AAP excludes video calls from their suggestion of zero screen time. If you let your child use technology, just make sure they are supervised, and you select the right content for them (National Childbirth Trust, 2019):

High quality TV programmes and apps aim to help toddlers with their language development, shape and colour recognition, numeracy and literacy. They also aim to promote problem solving, visual thinking and imagination. Educational apps are those that help toddlers learn these things in active, engaging, meaningful and socially interactive ways.

Dr. Vicki Hargraves, from The Education Hub, suggests all kinds of activities, such as digitally augmented doll houses or toys, drawing with an app, dancing to a song on YouTube, digitally altering their voice, or colouring through fun apps.

We also have digital books, Go-Pro cameras or apps that keep children playing outside, and so many more possibilities that allow children to expand their analogic experience through digital technology. “Many teachers and parents are cautious about play with screens in the early childhood context, but there is a broad array of potential opportunities for exploration and experimentation with digital activities” (Hargraves, 2022).

Always provide them with age-related digital play, look for hybrid games for the early years, and expand their possibilities as they grow up. Always supervise their digital play, and the youngest the child, the shorter the period they should spend straight on connected. In any case, make sure that they still get plenty of screen-free time, and that you turn off screens at least an hour before their bedtime.

As we have seen, any child can benefit from independent play, and it is something we adults need as well. As a final tip, consider their safety at all times. Remember that allowing them to play independently doesn’t mean they are unattended. Children will love to play in a safe environment where they feel supported, and you can check in on their play.

In the following chapter, we will share more ideas for encouraging a specific kind of play to help them unwind.

Chapter 5

Benefits of Calm Play

Running around in the outdoors, jumping up and down are great activities helping them get fit, active and get a good night sleep for toddlers and children. However, there are some moments children need to settle down: for example, right after having lunch, an hour before bedtime, or if they are recovering from a fever. In any case, while playing calmly, they can still maximise the benefits of play because even though your child may be calm and quiet, their brains are still active!

My children always struggled with this ‘calm play’ they loved to run, jump, be quite noisy, however calm play was always the last thing any of them wanted to do. They associated it with bedtime routines which wasn’t their favourite activity it meant the day is ending or as they saw it the fun was ending.

Here we will provide some tips for those moments of calm play. Some children adore them, while others are reluctant to sit down and stop bouncing against the walls, but they can all be engaged with the right motivation.

The Importance of Wind-Down Time

Healthy children are naturally energetic, and they love active play. Given the chance, they’ll spend most of their waking hours engaged in some kind of activity. However, most children don't realise when they get tired, and therefore become overtired. This can cause grumpiness, difficulties falling or remaining asleep, and in toddlers, temper tantrums. It's up to us, the parents, caregivers or the educators, to include some wind-down time in the child's routine, especially if they are no longer taking naps. A relaxing time during their day is also important if children become overstimulated or anxious (McIlroy, 2021):

> Sometimes, all they need is a change of pace or activity to calm their nerves or reset. While you can encourage activities such as breathing, closing your eyes or getting into a stretchy yoga pose, sometimes just a change of the type of activity will do the trick.

A child might resist these calm times if they feel all the fun is suddenly cut short. In order not to happen, I first of all suggest that instead of putting a sudden stop to their active play, you anticipate and prepare them for it: "Okay, you can take two more spins with your bike (or two more times down the slide, or chase your brother one last time), and then we should go inside." Offer them some attractive ideas for calm play, such as the ones listed in the sections below and try to make calm play part of their daily routines so it is expected by your child;

A bath is a great way for children to unwind. Some children don't like getting a bath, but in my experience, it is not the warm water and the scented soap that they reject, but the idea that playtime is over. Their bath time can be fun as well as relaxing. Try to keep some special toys they only use when playing in the tub. You can also blow bubbles, let them colour with washable bathtub markers, or lend them some empty bottles of shampoo to see if they float or fill them and empty them with water over and over again.

Before bedtime, some quiet games with music, reading stories, or hugging their favourite stuffed animal may help them create positive sleep associations that will make the transition to bedtime smoother. Anna Ranson, from the website The Imagination Tree, suggests using "the subtle power of lavender to induce calmness and sleepiness" (Ranson, 2014). You can implement it with a scented homemade dough, or a bowl of sensory rice or salt.

Another time when you can include calm play are car rides, especially if they are long. Between spending a lot of time sitting down, and the need to remain seated and buckled in their places, children tend to get bored and misbehave. Instead of simply relying on their tablets or lending them your mobile phones, try playing I spy, spotting cars of the same colour, singing a song from their playlist, or handing them some toys such as linking cubes or GeoStix® or listen to an audio story.

Cognitive Benefits of Independent, Calm Play

When you stimulate your children to play calmly, they are acquiring some valuable cognitive skills. First, they learn to concentrate and to self-soothe all those intense emotions that arise during active play. They learn that fun doesn't necessarily involve lots of adrenaline. Through calm activities such as puzzle-solving, they practise how to use logic, how to solve problems, and how to deal with frustration.

Calm play doesn't mean giving up on cooperative play. If you have two or more children, they can join up to set up a great teddy bear tea party or dress their dolls. Matching or sorting games are also great calm play. Make sure they are age-appropriate—they will give up soon if the activities are too hard for them, and they will get bored if they aren't challenging enough. If you are joining your child during their calm play or if siblings of different ages are playing together, they can also try building a puzzle with lots of pieces none of them could do by themselves.

For transition moments in early years and primary settings—for example, when children are waiting for tea time, or after coming from an exciting time at the playground—educators can rely on sensory stations as well as carpet games, such as riddles, Simon Says, I Spy, (McIlroy, 2021).

Calm time is also a great moment for practising their fine motor skills, cognitive development, resilience, persistence, curiosity, and learning-by-doing, such as:

Spooning (flour, sugar, rice, lentils, buttons, cereals, etc.)

Pouring, filling, and emptying (either liquids or sand)

Threading beans or noodles

Using their toy knife and fork with some playdough

Cutting and sticking papers, fabrics, stickers, autumn leaves, or crafting a collage from any other material you have

Simple sewing or knitting (for older children).

What if you are outdoors? Sure, if your children have been playing in the garden for an hour, and you know it's time for them to rest, hydrate, and relax for a while, you can always send them back inside. But in case you are spending all day at the beach, in the countryside, or on an excursion to a nearby forest, you can also propose some calm outdoor activities. For example:

1. Practice bird watching and finding insects.

Children can learn a lot about nature, and you can include a bird guide (a book or an app) to answer their questions about the habits of each species they spot. Try to ask them questions they can solve either by observing the birds or by doing some research later on: "Where does this bird live? Can you spot their nest? Is the bird alone or with its flock? What do you think they eat?" Of course, they have to remain quiet and still not scare the little bird away.

2. Ask them to find shapes in the clouds and tell a story in order to get them to lie on the ground and relax as they practise their verbal skills and use their imagination.

Try story telling with the clouds and shapes you see. This is a perfect activity for bonding with your child and enjoying some calm time yourself! When was the last time you lay on the grass and took a long, lasting look at the clouds?

3. Ask them to collect pebbles, leaves, or flowers (those already fallen on the ground so as not to damage the plants), sticks, pinecones, and so on.

You can make this interesting for preschoolers by adding numbers to the game: "Okay, so now I want you to pick six different stones! Now let's get leaves from five different trees." You can also encourage them to sort the collection by size, shape, or colour!

Music Is a Must!

Music can be used for both active play and wind down time. If you want your children to move around, they can dance, jump, or play. However, you can also use music for quiet activities. "Music is soothing for children and will immediately calm their nerves" (McIlroy, 2021).

Classical music is great, but you can also find plenty of instrumental versions of your favourite artists. There is also new-age music which can work well as the background of any calm play. If you want your child to listen and stay still, try giving them, earphones. Just make sure you set the volume low enough that they can hear you so there is no risk of ear damage.

There are plenty of calm play ideas that include music. Here are some:

> Turn off the lights in the room and give the children flashlights. Make the light circles "dance" to the rhythm of the music.
>
> Shadow puppets can be so much fun. You just need a torch, your fingers, and a good imagination. Use your fingers to make shapes in the light.

Draw a picture inspired by what they are hearing. It can be anything they like. If they draw concrete pictures, you can also encourage them to turn them into a story.

Give your children the supplies they need to craft and decorate their own musical instruments, such as homemade shakers filled with beans, drums made from cans, or handmade string instruments with elastic bands. The idea is not to get a perfect result but to explore where the sound comes from and have a great time while learning.

Nursery rhymes are a great resource for developing phonemic awareness, something that later will help them develop reading and writing skills. You can show them pictures of the rhymes, repeat them, create some different tunes for them.

An electric keyboard is a fantastic resource for learning the first notes. You can use colourful stickers to teach your children the notes and have sheet music with colours so they can learn their favourite song with a little practice! Remember to approach this learning with the positive parenting technique praising the process, "That's so fun to hear you are practising the keyboard, I love hearing you put in so much effort. I think I can already recognize that song."

Storytime and Books

Books are among the best calm activities for people of any age. From the time a baby is born, you can start reading to them. They are never too young to enjoy your lovely voice and to look at the colours of the pages. Once they can pick objects, books draw- their attention with their size and texture. Just remember babies and toddlers might chew paper books try cloth ones instead. Bonus you can wash them if they need it.

Toddlers have a blast naming some words, looking at the pictures, and learning to flip the pages. Even if they've moved on from the oral stage and no longer chew on the cardboard pages, I recommend you have a spare one of their favourite books in case they tear it apart from using it so much.

To create a conducive atmosphere to attract them to books, you can craft a reading corner or a "reading nook" with a soft lamp, sheets, and laundry pegs: "Toss in some cushions, blankets and a basket of books and they can lie down together to browse through them and rest their bodies" (Ranson, 2014). Children who can't read may still enjoy repeating the stories you told them so many times, perhaps adding some details of their own. Books spark their imagination and their creativity! I have countless pictures of my children that were inspired by book characters most of them from books with few or no pictures.

Read to your children. Read to them every day if possible. Make it fun and engaging by adding voices, gestures, sound effects, or by asking them questions even if they have listened to that story a few hundred times before. And, of course, make reading part of your night routines. "There's a reason bedtime stories exist as reading is one of the most calming things one can do before bedtime, even as an adult" (McIlroy, 2021). Audio stories can be another helpful resource for keeping children calm and entertained, but they should not replace quality time with a caregiver who reads to them and pays attention to their reactions, which makes a good story more enjoyable.

Colouring books are another good resource for calm time. Some of them, like watercolour books, allow children to explore different materials.

Mindfulness Magic

Among the many benefits practising mindfulness brings to children, worth mentioning are:

Better anxiety and stress management

- An increase in their attention span
- An increase in empathy through a better understanding and regulation of their as well as the others' emotions
- Body and sensorial awareness
- A stronger connection with nature.

Although this section does not refer specifically to playing, it provides a few simple mindfulness exercises you can teach your young children to help them improve their focus. After some minutes, they'll be able to calm their mind and better enjoy some of the quiet fun activities.

You can ask a child to perform certain movements with their body that will help them relieve the tension and become more at ease. Tanja McIlroy (2021) suggests the following exercises:

- Ask your child to stretch their toes forwards and backward while sitting on the floor with their legs stretched. Then, tell them to bend over and reach for their toes.
- Either standing up or sitting comfortably, ask them to shrug their shoulders, first the left one, then the right one and so on.

Tell them to stand up and pretend they are walking along a tightrope. If they are old enough, they can do it on tiptoes.

Rock themselves in a rocking chair, slower until the parent can't tell if they are really moving.

Imagine their belly is a balloon of their favourite colour. Breathe in and inflate the balloon. As they breathe out, tell them to imagine the air around them turning into that same colour.

Give them a glitter jar and ask them to shake it, then stare at it until everything settles.

Blow out a candle or a pinwheel. Place them further and further every time.

Do a child yoga class with the help of a video tutorial. It doesn't have to be long; ten minutes will do!

Ask your child to describe or draw their emotions.

After a couple of minutes performing one or two of these exercises, the child will be calmer and ready to accept your calm play ideas. These simple exercises can be implemented at home, in kindergarten, or at school.

Mindfulness can help children to self-regulate, and manage emotions, so when they make the transition to school they can deal with the more challenging environment. By getting children ready for the transition, caregivers can start to practise mindfulness with their children. Our next chapter is about helping them get ready for this new stage in their lives.

Chapter 6

School Readiness

A normal attention span is 3 to 5 minutes per year of a child's age. Therefore, a 2-year-old should be able to concentrate on a particular task for at least 6 minutes, and a child entering kindergarten should be able to concentrate for at least 15 minutes. Children are naturally curious and love to explore and experiment with new activities. Therefore, it is imperative to seek out games or simple play activities that can increase a child's attention span.

As toddlers grow, their games gain in complexity. Playing can help them to acquire tools that will be valuable once they start kindergarten or school. This is a huge change in their lives! Especially for children who were locked down during the pandemic, returning to school has been a challenge no matter their age (Mundy, 2021):

> Merging evidence suggests that the pandemic, and all its associated restrictions, are having a negative impact upon children's emotional well-being. We know that anxiety stifles curiosity. If we are going to help children transition back into school and all the learning opportunities that it offers, the first thing we need to focus upon is their social and emotional well-being.

Again, play has a crucial part to play in helping your child adjust to such a significant change. "Play can assist children in adjusting to a school setting. It enhances children's learning readiness and their cognitive development by allowing them to move from subject and area without the fear of failure" (Anderson-McNamee and Bailey, 2010).

Is your child emotionally ready for school? How can you help them through play to acquire some basic milestones and make the transition easier for all? Once in school, how can educators include play into the daily activities to enhance the learning process as well as the emotional adjustment of their students?

Getting Ready for School?

Most people in the UK start school age 4, Australia 5 and USA 5, whereas most European countries is 6. While most parents decide to enrol their child in school based on their school age, this is an indicator but by no means the only one, nor even the most important. They need to be emotionally ready to start school. This includes being socially ready to deal with situations that will put them out of their comfort zone. They should know they are in a safe, supportive environment to take calculated risks which may be as small as pouring water in messy play, climbing in the playground, or building the tallest tower with the blocks.

To make that big decision based on your child's personal needs, you should pay attention to other facts too: "There are some key indicators that can help you to decide. Your child's paediatrician and preschool staff are also good sources that can help you gauge when your child is ready" (Rock, 2022). Here are some questions to consider:

Is your child toilet trained? Some schools request that they are able to use the toilet independently before they start. There are many different approaches to toilet training. But like walking, talking, and other milestones, each child develops at their own pace, and it is hard to potty train children that are not ready or physically mature.

Can you understand what your child says? Teachers and classmates are great sources of verbal interactions, and thus, being in kindergarten may help a child develop their language skills. However, if your child can't communicate even their basic thoughts and wishes, they may have a hard time at school.

Can they follow directions? We know all children sometimes do as they please and not as they are told. But does your child have the ability to at least understand and follow simple tasks, such as sitting in a specific place, following the teacher, or performing everyday activities with some independence?

How do they interact with other children? Is your child used to being with their peers in the playground? Do they have other children to play with, even if they haven't reached the associative play stage yet? To be in a class with 10-15 or even

30 other children, you must know that your child can at least tolerate them.

What about separation anxiety? If your child has serious difficulties being without you or another caregiver, adaptation to school/nursery will take longer. Maybe it's better to help them overcome this stage before sending them to school.

Are they going through other huge changes in their lives? If you have just had a baby, moved to a new home, or divorced, maybe starting school could be challenging. If possible, let them go through one big adaptation at a time.

School readiness is about children, but it is also about parents/caregivers being ready to send their children back to an educational environment. So here are a few tips for parents/caregivers to get your children ready:

> Empower your child to make choices, even if it is just the colour paint to use or which way to walk home, what to wear.
>
> Allow time for unstructured free play. Make them feel safe, and supported, and help them to learn through experiences and play. Play-based learning builds children's confidence, motor skills, cognitive development, and social and emotional skills. It is a fun and engaging way for parents and caregivers to engage with children.

Children may be anxious and feel apprehensive due to the many changes happening in such a short period. Listen to the stories of how your child reflects on their day and give them experiences from going to the park, try different activities with them, such as engaging in their play, and then discuss how they feel about going to school.

In the early years as a parent, you should focus on their well-being rather than academic learning. Children naturally love to play and explore their environment. Parents/caregivers can prepare their children for school by starting to implement routines for meals, taking turns, listening, and unstructured play and by focusing on the positives from spending time together, in a play-based environment.

Importance of Taking Risks

If a child enters school or kindergarten and is afraid of making a mistake, their experience will be terrifying, or at least, they'll miss out on all kinds of positive experiences. Children should know that school is about learning, and that you learn by making mistakes.

This can mean, for young children attending kindergarten for the first time, that it doesn't matter if they spill the water paint or if they colour outside the lines. Of course, you can create this confidence from the start by letting them engage in all kinds of scooping, threading, transferring, and classifying activities and not making a big deal if they do something wrong. For example, if they are transferring coloured liquids from one big glass into a small one, and some of the liquid spills, you can help them realise why that happens. You can also get them a rag and let them clean up their mess. It's all part of the learning process!

For older children, this can mean encouraging them to ask questions and to come up with answers by themselves, instead of providing them with an effortless solution. Praise your child's curiosity rather than their knowledge. If you congratulate your child after asking a great question, you are teaching them you value their curiosity. Instead of simply googling the answer, help them solve the problem by asking even more questions.

For example, when working in the garden, let's say your child asks if a flower in a pot needs to be watered every day. Instead of searching the answer on a gardening website, you could go, "That's a great question! I wonder what we should do to find out. What do you think happens to a plant if they get too much water? And what if they get too little? Well, what could we do to decide?"

Of course, there is a chance that the plant in question may fade before the child comes up with the right answer. In that case, don't blame them, show them what they learned from the experience, and help them plant a new flower. This shows them it's okay to make mistakes and to take risks!

"Be a Good Sport"

Attending school means that the play will not revolve only around your child's needs. Instead, they need to start sharing spaces and elements, work on taking turns, and eventually, play by the rules (Anderson-McNamee & Bailey, 2010):

> When children move from a self-centred world to an understanding of the importance of social contracts and rules, they begin to play games with rules. Part of this development occurs when they learn games such as Follow the Leader, Simon Says, and team sports. Games with rules teach children the concept that life has rules that everyone must follow.

Of course, once your child begins playing ruled games, that means they also learn the difference between winning and losing. It is something they need to learn because not everything in life will go their way. Someday, an employer will choose someone else despite your child having a spotless CV. Someday, a person they are attracted to will say "no" when they ask them out, even if they do so politely.

Someday, the bank may deny them credit. And learning to deal with not coming first or even losing or failing is an important lesson. There will come a time when they will fail a test.

Your child needs to accept that they can't win all the time. This is why competitive games and learning to follow rules are important. However, putting too much emphasis on the result will mean that the child loses sight of the intrinsic pleasure of play. This is why the concept of being "a good sport" is so important: You have to accept a negative result with a positive attitude. In the same way, you have to help others, so if you do win, you have to empathise with the other players and don't make fun of them or brag about their victory.

Parents teach children about good sportsmanship through example, first of all. Take an honest look at yourself and make sure you are a good role model: For example, when you are watching a match on television, you can make good comments about the rival's team if they do a great play, you can speak respectfully of your rivals when you lose, and you can avoid making excuses when you mess up somehow.

Elaine Taylor-Klaus, from the blog Impact Parents, suggests engaging in conversations with your children on the importance of being a good sport, setting realistic expectations about the possibility of winning or losing before the game begins, and encouraging each child to compete with themselves: “Encourage siblings to root for each other and try not to foster a competitive environment among the family. If it is a competitive family, it's a great place to practise keeping it friendly and supportive” (Taylor-Klaus, 2022).

Both winning and losing teaches important life lessons: “While winning gives your child a sense of pride and control, there are still benefits that come with experiencing defeat” (Toth, 2014). When playing a simple rule-based game with your child that mostly depends on chance, you can seize that opportunity to display your empathy while at the same time you don’t sugar coat the harsh reality of losing by saying things such as “It’s pure luck,” or “It’s no big deal.” Instead, you can say something like you understand their disappointment, but the truth is that things don’t always work out the way we expect them to.

At the same time, when more strategic games are already part of your child’s play, and they lose, this is a great chance to turn their frustration into improving their problem-solving skills (Toth, 2014):

> Say something indirect like, “Hmm, I wonder what would've happened if you'd moved this chess piece instead.” This way, your child won't feel you're being critical. Plus, she’ll be more likely to remember a new strategy if she draws her own conclusions.

Competitive games are also great for teaching perseverance

(before starting to play, explain to your child it's not okay to simply "give up" when they find out the other player is winning), and self-confidence (by praising their right plays despite the outcome of the game).

All of these valuable resources will come in handy once your child enters school, not only when it comes to social interaction in the playground or when practising a sport during physical education class, but also for when it comes time for tests and exams.

School and Home Learning

In this last section of the chapter, we'll compare two possible approaches to schooling, list the advantages of each one, and give some tips on how educators can include more play into their daily activities, whether children attend a traditional school or are home schooled.

School

When we think about traditional schooling we are referring to sending your child to study in an environment different from their home, surrounded by other children of the same age, and tutored by a professional of education. Of course, there is a wide variety of so-called "traditional" schools, and the experience of a child attending a religious boarding school may have little to do with a child whose parents sign them into a Montessori school or a Waldorf school.

In any case, some of the advantages we should mention are the following:

> The children have the guidance of a highly trained professional in education (their teacher), who has not only a degree in their subject but also theoretical and practical knowledge of pedagogy. Parents or caregivers whom teach their children at home may be well-meaning, however at the same time, will have to be prepared for the challenges with home learning.
>
> Children interact with their peers daily. Even conflicts and friendships are opportunities to guide children to become part of society: "Working with their peers on a daily basis can teach a lot of valuable lessons, such as teamwork and cooperation, conflict resolution, diplomacy, and other vital social skills" (Kensington, 2019).
>
> Having children at school means parents can work on their careers. In many cases, parents, caregivers need to work for children to be at school.

> Any school will offer structure; children generally thrive on routine and schools often offer a steady safe routine for many children.

According to Dr. Sarah Mundy, Consultant Clinical Psychologist and Author of Parenting Through Stories, the pandemic didn't help the current education. Teachers are pressured to help their students "catch up," and sometimes this means overlooking the importance of play in the classroom (2021). It's not only the parents who should put their focus on the children's well-being rather than on their grades, but the same applies to educators, especially now: "A child who is anxious about change and with worries about his friendships is much less likely to engage in their times tables" (Mundy, 2021). Mundy provides some useful tips teachers can implement in their classrooms:

> Many children feel overloaded with sensory stimulation as they return to a loud, crowded classroom, teachers should provide them more access to outside play to keep them calm and to give them a sensory break.
>
> Some children experienced regressions and are suffering from the corresponding pressure, offering them play resources that would normally be considered for younger children may also help them.
>
> Breaktimes are especially important and should be prioritised. They offer plenty of learning

> opportunities and the practice of social skills. "Children develop a sense of self, learn to interact with other children, how to make friends, and the importance of role-playing. Exploratory play in school allows children time to discover and manipulate their surroundings" (Anderson-McNamee & Bailey, 2010).

Home Learning

Although home schooling or home learning use to be a privilege to a select few, in the past years it has gained popularity. Even before the pandemic, almost 50,000 children were home schooled in Britain (Kensington, 2019), and in the United States, the numbers are even more impressive, with over 2 million home schooled children and the number increasing up to an annual 15% (Barrington, 2022). These families take a much bigger active role in their children's education, and they choose this method because it has some advantages compared to a traditional school:

> It allows parents and children to focus on their preferred topics and subjects of study, and they can learn at their own pace.

It offers more flexible timetables, to better adjust to the family's lifestyle. Plus, it cuts down commuting times and costs.

It allows parents and children to spend more time together. "Some families also believe that this strengthens the bond between parent and children, as more time is spent together during the formative years" (Kensington, 2019)

It may be the best choice for children who are struggling to keep up with their peers, have special needs, or suffer a great deal from anxiety at school.

It's a great opportunity for learning through direct experiences, as many parents take children to libraries, museums, parks, and other trips. School trips aren't nearly as frequent!

It's also the choice for some religious families who want to give their children more time for their faith-based education.

When it comes to including play in your child's home learning program, this is also one of the main strengths. "In the world of learning at home, as parents and caregivers, we can supercharge their non-classroom experience and complement the school time learning. This presents a great opportunity" (Welch, 2021). As a parent who is involved in their child's home learning, make sure whatever topic or subject you approach, you give your child plenty of opportunities to learn by playing.

Whether you send your child to a traditional school or choose to home school them, play is a crucial part of the learning process. "Numerous studies have shown that children who have been taught through play-based learning have a more positive attitude to learning, a wider vocabulary and advanced problem solving, lateral thinking and analytical skills" (Welch, 2021).

In our next chapter, we'll take a closer look at how certain life challenges arise during play, and how we can seize on them as opportunities for giving our children valuable tools.

Chapter 7

What *We* Learn from Children's Play

As teachers we learn so much from the children we have taught over the years; as parents we learn so much watching our own children. From how they are feeling in each moment to their interests, development stages, friends and how they react to situations, when they feel overwhelmed or excited.

So far, we have explored a wide range of ways in which children learn without realising when they play. However, if we pay attention to what's going on and we watch them play, we can also learn a lot about them. When children play, they tend to be more open and communicative about their day, about their feelings, or about a problem they haven't solved yet. Through play, issues such as sibling rivalry, competence, lack of confidence, or childhood fears may arise, and we can seize this opportunity and help children move through their issues.

Crucial Importance of Role-Playing

Role-playing is any activity in which the child recreates a situation and plays an active part of a specific character in its development—it can happen during independent play as well as in social play. Whether they are setting the table, playing to drive a car by holding a toy steering wheel while sitting on the dining room table, or pretending it's their turn to put mum or dad to bed and to read or make up a bedtime story. In all these situations the child acts as someone else. By fitting into this new role, or recreating real-life situations during their play, they get a better understanding of their surrounding reality (Huleatt, 2018):

> Role-play is how children make sense of their world, acting out experiences, ideas, or stories. Imagination, which is at the heart of children's role-play, is more important than knowledge according to Albert Einstein, "for knowledge is limited, whereas imagination embraces the entire world."

Children engage in different types of role-plays, and we'll describe the most common (Vivvi, 2021).

Real-Life Situations Role-Play

This is the kind of play in which children re-enact everyday moments through their play. They can pretend to be themselves going through past experiences (such as recreating a holiday by the beach, or getting an X-ray at the hospital), or being someone else, thus allowing themselves to express new thoughts or emotions: "Will is not afraid of the ocean, but I'm Eddie, and Eddie won't go into the sea!"

This type of role-play allows them to learn from the real

world, enhancing their language skills, and practising empathy. Parents or caregivers can learn a lot about how children see us by observing this play, as well as understanding their fears and worries. For example, if a child is afraid of the dark, they can manifest it's their doll who is scared. You can take part in the play and ask the doll why she is so scared and ask the child for possible solutions to "help the doll" overcome their fears.

Sometimes children don't recreate past experiences but anticipate future ones. "When children act out life's problems in pretend-playing, it helps them cope with the struggles in their own ways. It also provides a safe opportunity for children to rehearse skills and future social roles" (Li, 2022). This role-play is a chance to explore their inner self and deal with changes: a new sibling who is about to be born, a new school, moving house.

Again, children show their feelings through play, and you will see and hear them recalling situations they had to deal with during their day or week, etc. This is when we can join the play and ask open-ended questions to help them understand and give them strategies to manage their feelings.

Occupational Role-Play

Sometimes children enjoy pretending to be public figures of authority in their surroundings (police officer, firefighter, doctor, or a vet), or they can pretend to be the adults surrounding them (such as being the teacher and their dolls being the students, being the parent, and the younger sibling being the baby, and so on).

In any case, this role-play allows them to feel empowered: "When children pretend to be police officers, doctors, nurses, teachers, or construction workers, they foster empathy amongst their peers. Imagining yourself in a high-profile position in society is a fun and helpful pastime for young people" (The Little Dreamers Nursery, 2022). As a parent or an educator, pay attention and see if a child dramatically changes their personality when acting out: Perhaps they are trying to change some aspect of their behaviour or abilities—being brave, fast, having other people listening to them—and so far, they can only achieve it during play. "Children who are normally quiet may 'talk' on the phone as part of their role-play" (Huleatt, 2018).

There are many other benefits from this kind of role-play. Children can learn concepts, such as the importance of money, quantities, similarities, and differences by playing games such as the restaurant or the supermarket. They also get to practise their manners—saying "please" and "thank you"—and social skills, such as exchanging roles and taking turns.

Fantasy Role-Play

"Imagination is intrinsic to role-play as children represent their ideas, thoughts, and feelings through their play" (Huleatt, 2018). Fantasy is the kind of role-play that expands the child's imagination the most. When you see your child representing their favourite movie character, someone that can be a princess, a superhero, a being from another world, or even a villain, they are boosting their creativity, their verbal skills, and their gross motor skills by jumping, running, and climbing. At the same time, they are learning about concepts, such as differentiating right from wrong, the importance of teamwork, empathy (while trying to give their character motivation), and negotiating with their peers (The Little Dreamers Nursery, 2022):

> While playing a role they love might inspire confidence and courage, it can also create new ideas and concepts. [...] In the early years of life, role-playing teaches children how to negotiate character roles, such as who is good or who is evil in a situation. Negotiation is frequently the only way they can get their first option, but they can find a workable solution by working together as a group.

When you see your child actively engaged in role-play, try to listen without intervening. Only once the play is over (because we don't want to interrupt it or condition it), you can seize the opportunity to speak to your child about the differences between fantasy and reality, which parts of their play have a correlation in the real world and which ones only happen in movies and stories.

Finally, fantasy role-play is a great way for children to find tools to deal with some common childhood fears such as monsters, witches, ghosts, and other creatures that frighten them in their nightmares. By confronting them during play, and reasoning about how they are not real, they get resources for getting over their terrors. However, if your child often displays this kind of fear, you may want to find out what is triggering their fear. Have they indivertibly been exposed to something on a screen that is inappropriate for their age.

Recreating and Overcoming Difficulties

Playing can help children overcome all sorts of childhood difficulties—as well as provide their parents and their educators with valuable tools to help them. Whether the child uses the play to manifest their feelings, or if the conflict arises during play, every case provides a precious opportunity to speak up their minds and find useful strategies to deal with the conflict. Here we will go to some common situations most children may bump into at some point.

Children with Emotional Dysregulation

One of my own children really struggled with self-regulation he had emotional dysregulation. This is an area we have worked with them through play for a while to help when they feel overwhelmed, identifying trigger points, being able to calm down with a caregiver or even without. One of the most effective ways that worked for us at home and in the classroom was understanding they had a safe space that they could go to before the feelings arose and being part of an emotional support program where we discuss different emotions, talk about scenarios, reasons why we find it hard.

Children, especially the ones who have been diagnosed with ADHD or have lived through some sort of childhood trauma, experience and manifest their emotions outside the normally accepted range. They may display sudden bursts of anger or break into tears, high levels of shame, frequent mood swings, etc. "Being emotionally dysregulated means a person feels emotions more intensely than they should, feels them for longer than they should, feels them at inappropriate times, or responds to them in extreme ways" (Cummings, 2020). These children have trouble managing their emotions, and this can create repercussions for their social behaviour as well. This symptom requires treatment, and in children, therapy is preferred to medication.

Play can benefit children by helping them self-regulate their emotions. We can offer them more tools to empower them, help them gain control of their feelings and the way they express them. Occupational therapist Sarah Shakibaie, from Ready Kids, suggests some fun games such as emotion and situation game boards, emotional twister, or emotional charades (all of them aiming at the child recognizing and putting names to their, as well as others', emotions). Shakibaie also insists on the power of music for self-soothing: "Music can begin a conversation about emotions which lead to emotion regulation" (Shakibaie, 2021).

Sensory play allows children to feel less overwhelmed by their emotions because exploring the materials helps them focus on the present moment. Role-play is also a great resource for regulating their emotions: "Make-believe play is especially important now as it helps little ones process their fears, act them out, and therefore communicate their inner world. Play here is a type of therapy–they can release their stress through play" (Faure, 2021). In any case, play (especially free play) provides children with a much-needed sense of control, safety, and calmness.

Managing Sibling Rivalry

Having 3 siblings, being fortunate enough to have a twin there was always a little rivalry however also a lot of love underneath as well. I'll always remember as a twin we would argue, however if anyone came in between us we would both join forces. Our parents originally called us thunder and lightning being the youngest of 4 in 5 years it was indeed a busy, chaotic childhood. However, on reflection the experiences both positive and negative we had together were many lessons learnt for everyone.

Anyone who has a brother, or a sister has experienced sibling rivalry to some degree. "Sibling rivalry is an inevitable challenge of raising more than one child. No matter what the age difference or personalities of the children, sooner or later, every child with siblings gets upset with their brother or sister" (Merali & Orson, 2016).

However, this doesn't mean we should get used to children not getting along and fighting, arguing, or nagging each other the whole time! It can be exhausting for parents to be referees, and the whole atmosphere of the home can change when children constantly compete for their parents' attention.

According to Paediatrician Sigmund Norr, MD, sibling rivalry is inevitable because it is due to factors such as age order, the temperament of each child, and the family dynamics, not because one child receives the best toy for Christmas or gets to eat the largest piece of pizza. But sibling rivalry is also manageable: "There is no way to stop the bickering forever, but there are many ways to minimize conflict and to maximize productive resolution. Start with small changes" (Cleveland Clinic, 2020). Some ways parents can prevent sibling rivalry is by keeping their calm, avoiding comparisons while at the same time celebrating individual differences, and treating children fairly.

When parents organise engaging activities together, such as going to fun places, or creating special family rituals (how about pizza night every Thursday?), they also contribute to strengthening the bond between their children by making them share beautiful memories and giving them something in common rather than something to fight about. It's great to play as a family. However, it is also important to dedicate time to each sibling (Anderson-McNamee & Bailey, 2010):

> Try to spend individual time with each of your children. When a parent or sibling plays a board game with a child, shares a bike ride, plays baseball, or reads a story, the child learns self-importance. Your child's self-esteem gets a boost.

Overcoming Shyness through Play

Children, as well as adults, have different personalities, and just because a child isn't talkative doesn't mean they have a problem. However, when their shyness becomes an obstacle and a child isn't enjoying playdates, birthday parties, or even going to school, then we have to address it because it's not just a personality trait, but a sign of social anxiety.

The first thing parents must do is address their children's problems and avoid labelling them as "shy" or "introverted". Talk to your child in a safe environment and try to avoid the conversation being an interrogatory: Simply let them talk about how they are feeling and encourage them to write those feelings down as a list (Ireland, 2015). Practising some of the mindful techniques we explained before in Chapter 5, and anticipating future situations may help the child get in touch with their feelings and acknowledge their anxiety.

Arts and crafts are great play resources for shy children, and they can be implemented both at home or school: "Creating a common workspace for kids to work in groups helps a lot in school. Sharing crafting supplies and a workstation is sufficient to help the kid to learn how to interact with others" (NSN, 2022). At the same time, both parents, as well as teachers, should keep encouraging shy children to take part in oral activities. The adult should guide the child with an example by always introducing themselves and greeting them to help them gain confidence. Games that increase the child's natural curiosity, as good as outdoor free play, can also help shy children overcome their anxiety.

Improving Schoolwork Through Play

Many children face academic challenges at some point. Besides listening to their teacher's advice, you can increase their learning skills through appropriate games. There is a wide variety of STEAM toys that stimulate children's natural curiosity and eagerness to learn. They are fun for all ages, and you don't need your child to struggle in school for them to enjoy them.

Some children have a hard time in mathematics. Counting, stacking, abacus, dice games, or classifying toys can increase their maths skills, as well as playing games that involve counting money (it can be a board game but it can also be an occupational role-play, such as playing supermarket with toy money and a cash register). math games, number trains, or number puzzles are great for working with number recognition. Blocks and tiles are great for helping them understand patterns.

When it comes to literacy, of course, you want to provide your child with all kinds of attractive and varied books of all shapes and sizes and encourage them to read by using some of the tips already provided in Chapter 5. Phonics toys allow them to explore the sounds of the language. You can make learning fun by playing games (depending on the learning stage of your child, you may choose letter bingos or sight word games), spelling or rhyming puzzles, sets of flashcards, words or letter magnets, or interactive books.

As for digital play, there are thousands of applications that are specifically designed for learning. Just make sure the tablet or the mobile phone doesn't replace other kinds of play but complements them, and that you supervise the use of electronic devices.

Finally, whatever area your child is struggling with, make sure you also leave them plenty of time to do things they are good at, to boost their self-esteem. To improve their weaker areas, they must become confident in their capacities. What can be better for that than praising them for what they know they enjoy and do well?

By the time children spend most of their playtime in cooperative play, they are mature enough to follow and understand the rules of a game. It can be something as simple as "Duck, duck, goose", or it can be as complex as chess! In any case, structured games empower, inspire, motivate, and engage pre-schoolers and older children alike.

Structured Play and Its Benefits

Unlike free play, structured play is an activity that has a goal. It doesn't need to be competitive, as the goal may be common among the different players. And it includes activities as simple as tag or hide-and-seek, and as complex as practising sports. Board games are another example of structured play, and we'll turn to them later on.

Free play, we have already seen, offers plenty of advantages for children's development, but so does structured play. They get to explore and socialise, gain confidence, and they also can learn from their mistakes (Ewing, 2020):

> There's a lot of emphasis placed on a child's developing logic skills. It challenges them to follow directions and solve problems that come up along the way. It also provides "structure" by establishing guidelines and rules that are used to achieve the goal of the activity.

Here are some values your child can cultivate when being engaged in structured play:

Perseverance. Because these games have a goal, you keep playing them until you achieve it, or until every player decides to call it a day. Consider the following example: Your child, who is independently playing with their magnetic tiles, has decided to build a spacecraft, but it's difficult, so they change their mind and continue building something entirely different. However, during structured play, your child is playing with friends or siblings, and even though the goal might be more challenging than they thought at first, because they all share it, they encourage each other to keep going, until they achieve it.

Active listening. When they play a structured game, someone explains the rules. Your child needs to make sure they understand them, ask any necessary questions, or even negotiate some of the instructions. In any case, "as a child spends more time engaging in structured activities, they will gradually learn that listening and paying attention to directions are the keys to a successful outcome" (Ewing, 2020).

A sense of accomplishment. When children achieve a specific goal (jumping on one foot up to the top of hopscotch, running faster than their chaser, and reaching the "safe spot" in time), they feel empowered and happy. They don't even need to win the game to achieve that sense of triumph.

Problem-solving. It's directly linked to perseverance. If a goal isn't easy to achieve at first, the child has to think outside the box and come up with new strategies on how to get through. They can also learn by watching how other children deal with the same difficulties through different approaches.

Time for Board Games

For those of you who have struggled to engage in free play with a toddler or pretending to be a princess with a pre-schooler, you may actually start having fun when your child is old enough play board games with your children. There's a reason why board games are popular among teenagers and adults as well as children. In fact, one of the main benefits of playing board games is that the whole family can become involved and *play*, not just with the child and for the child's sake, but because you want to.

However, when you play with your children "it's important to choose games that are appropriate for your child's developmental stage. Look for themes that they are interested in and consider complexity and the amount of time it takes to play the game" (Welch, 2022a). When your pre-schooler starts playing board games, a "4-in-line" may be complex enough. But when choosing a game for a schoolchild, something too simple will bore them quickly, and something too complex may frustrate them. Luckily, "most games now publish the rules online, so it is easy to have a look through to make sure if a game is going to be complex enough or too complex for your audience"

Here are some of the main cognitive, social, and emotional advantages board games offer for children:

Focus. Because children have fun while playing a board game, they increase their attention span. This is one reason board games are especially recommended for children who are energetic and find it hard to spend time sitting down. Board games are a great idea as a calm activity, and you can even play them at night because, unlike screens, they won't affect a child's sleeping pattern. Quite the contrary, playing can help your child wind down.

Motivation. Of course, we want to emphasise having fun and not winning, but the truth is that deep down, even we want that little taste of achievement that comes when beating someone in a board game, right? "Competition encourages kids to try hard as they find their '*honour*' at stake. Whether they are playing Catan Junior or Dixit, they tend to be more focused on winning" (Davidson, 2017).

Decision making. If you are playing Goose Game or Snakes and Ladders, it's all about how the dice turn. But as children grow up, they can begin playing strategic board games that involve making decisions, trying to figure out the adversary's new move, and learning from their mistakes to play better next time.

Impulse control. Playing board games also teaches children not to react. If they throw a temper tantrum and the chips start flying around the room, the game is over! You can talk to your child and help them deal with their feelings of frustration, and to think before they act. The recommendations on how to be a good sport that we already explained in Chapter 6 apply here as well. However, board games teach impulse control not only in the case the child loses but also for thinking before making a move while developing a strategy.

Moral decisions. Board games can also be a great source of life lessons. For instance, a child may feel the impulse to cheat or break a rule to win. In this case, you can explain to them why cheating is wrong and how it removes all the satisfaction of winning a game. Some complex games, such as Catan™ or Carcassonne™, also put players in the position of choosing who to favour and who to punish. Younger children are not mature enough to play them, but for older ones is a great exercise in not taking things personally.

Some parents wonder if it's okay to let the child win, or even allow them to "cheat" in innocent ways, such as miscounting when moving their chip on a board. Although it might be tempting to always let a child win, it is way more valuable to give them the tools to deal with their frustration and losing in a safe supportive environment. You can focus on the fun you are having playing than the results.

With games that depend on pure luck, you can apply some changes to the rules to give children a chance (for example, they get to throw the dice twice if they get a low number). Set these rules beforehand. If older children are playing and they complain, explain to them the difference between equal treatment and fair treatment we already established before.

With strategy games, you can "let them win" but not by playing wrong on purpose. Instead, play while explaining what you are doing and anticipating your future moves. For instance, if you are playing 4-in-line, you can ask them, "Why do you think I placed this chip in that row? What should you do next? What happens if you don't cover this row?" You may also allow them to redo a movement if the latter caused them to lose the game, but only after they find out how they can improve the result based on logic, not simply guessing. This way, their winning is a result of critical thinking, not of you underestimating them and lowering down your level.

Chapter 8

Benefits of Play for Children With Special Education Needs (SEN)

Playing benefits every single child in so many ways. When it comes to children with Special Education Needs, they have a lot to gain from play, especially from sensory toys. In this last chapter, we will approach the different ways children that are neurodiverse with autism spectrum disorder (ASD), ADHD as well as children with other special needs, can find in play a way towards inclusion, understanding, and overall happiness among their classmates as well as their siblings. The role of the parent and/or the educator is key in creating an inclusive play environment, in which differences aren't merely *tolerated*, but embraced as a part of human diversity that enriches us all. As caregivers we need to remember that our children's ability is their superpower.

Play in the Autism Spectrum Disorder

When we talk about autism as a "spectrum," it's because people with autism can experience it in a wide variety of ranges. Generally, Autism is described as a disorder because of the challenges in social interaction, sometimes accompanied by some grade of difficulties in verbal communication (that can vary from not talking at all, to having trouble understanding irony or drawing inferences from the other person's speech). Most children with autism also display repetitive or restricted behaviours. Besides, "children and adults with autism can have sensory processing issues, which may make other people feel that they are not present, or in the moment".

Because of these traits, children with autism—and their parents—suffer when they struggle to find playmates because they don't quite *fit* into other children's ideas of play. They prefer sorting games, and repetitive tasks, and they soon display a really strong interest in a specific field (some children are fascinated by numbers, while others like maps, or talk exclusively about dinosaurs). They prefer to engage in solitary play and sometimes seem uninterested in other children.

They don't usually engage in role-play or symbolic play: "Children with autism rarely develop pretend play skills without help. They may enjoy placing toy trains on a track. But they're unlikely to enact scenes or make sound effects unless they are actively taught and encouraged to do so" (Rudy, 2022). And because of their difficulties with verbal interactions, they also keep away from cooperative play.

Still, children with an autism spectrum disorder can and will play, and benefit from this activity like any other child, but parents and educators must consider their unique qualities and challenges. With the guidance and the proper intervention of adults, children with an autism spectrum disorder can engage in parallel play. Older children that have acquired enough verbal skills can also play structured games (although, unlike other children, they insist on following the set of rules by the book).

One great way to include a child with autism in play is through sensory toys. "Sensory play help children on the spectrum because they can help them focus and pay attention, plus they can also help relieve some of their stress and anxiety making them relax, focus and calm" Through the use of sensory toys, these children find relief from the over-stimulation of everyday activities. Some of the toys you can use are already within your reach, such as making bubbles, playing with sand and water, or making a homemade sensory bottle for them to look at when they need to find inner peace. All of these toys help them calm down by focusing and refining their motor skills. Additionally, when shared with other children, these toys can also increase their self-confidence and promote verbal and social skills.

Maths toys can be popular for children within the spectrum, because of their preference for sorting, counting, and repeating activities. Through geometrical tiles, rainbow pebbles, GeoStix™, linking cubes, or counters, you can help a child with autism show their main strengths and share their interest with other children.

Most children with autism benefit more from structured play than from free play, because while too much stimulation makes them lose focus and feel overwhelmed, having a goal and a limited number of options may help them concentrate and engage in play for long periods.

Children with Special Needs

Other children need special approaches to play as well. No matter what their ability is, every child can learn and have fun at their own pace. They all deserve to be loved, respected, and appreciated for their individuality.

Our role as parents or educators is to make each child feel included and special! Here, we will briefly address some inclusive ideas for children with SEN to feel part of the team, to learn without realising, and to have fun when interacting with other children. How can we help them overcome their difficulties and enjoy playtime the most? One of my own children has always had trouble with self-regulation when he is feeling overwhelmed.

Attention Deficit Hyperactivity Disorder (ADHD)

Children with ADHD often have difficulty with attention and regulation. They demonstrate emotional dysregulation, hyperactivity, hyperfocus and impulsivity, which can affect planning, organising, communicating, and managing behaviour from the parent or caregivers' perspective. While it's most noticeable among children with ADHD, all children need a supportive, safe space to learn. Children bloom in an environment which caters to the needs of the individual, with teachers who believe that all children have the capacity and capability to perform well.

One of the quick wins a parent or caregiver can have in a class or at home with Children with ADHD is to allow for movement. Maybe a fidget or Pop It toy, maybe running an errand in between tasks, maybe moving to a 'safe place' when unsettled. Allow them a safe space to decompress, they may have been holding it in all day. Then need to release all the energy when they get home. Find a way for your child to decompress.

With rewards for children with ADHD we talk about 'gamification' and 'levelling up', where parents or caregivers help children take small steps to win "a place on the rainbow", or win "a pot of gold". But direct, clear instructions, peppered with praise for effort has always worked, especially on children with ADHD.

A focus on learning through play or hands on learning, allowing for experimentation and exploration, is a great way for children with ADHD to gain confidence and a sense of reward in a classroom environment. Grounding a positive experience of the learning environment in the primary years is all-important for better long-term educational outcomes for children with ADHD.

Understanding Self Regulation for Children

Earlier we discussed helping children through emotional dysregulation through play. Let's go further in understanding self-regulation for Children. There are many ways to look at why children are finding it hard to self-regulate. Understanding the 5 domains of self-regulations will help caregivers look past the behaviour and why it occurs in individuals to helping them manage it.

The domain are separate systems but also interlinked with each other. If you are considering why a child is showing signs of stress it is important to consider all five domains to form a complete picture; this can help us to find out what they are trying to express through their behaviour.

1. The biological domain – factors such as nutrition, amount of sleep, physical exercise, state of health, level of energy and sensory inputs

affect stress and therefore behaviour. Are they hungry, tired, hot, cold, hypo or hyper sensitive to sensory input.

2. The emotional domain – this refers to the individual's ability to evaluate and modify their emotions being able to self-regulate. Is your child over excited, having negative emotions, feeling overwhelmed.
3. The cognitive domain – this refers to the individual's ability to remain focused, maintain concentration and their ability to switch from task to task. Does your child have a poor working memory, lack of attention, easily distracted, confused this can all lead not being able to self regulate.
4. The social domain – this involves looking at the impact the individual and their behaviour and actions are having on others. Can they not understand or act on social cues, tones of voice.
5. The prosocial domain – this involves positive behaviours that enable an individual to have friendships, social acceptance and empathy. Do they understand other people's strong emotions, stress or even a sense of injustice. This domain is strongly related to the other four domains.

There are many ways Parents & Caregivers can support children in managing their emotional responses include, many of these we still use with my child who has always struggled with his emotional responses.

Helping them to identify the emotion and find ways to delay it, such as using calming techniques, finding a safe space, or taking time out, etc. in response to anger, frustration, feeling overwhelmed or anxiety. Calming techniques might include deep breathing or counting, for example.

- Identify a safe space. This could be a space created for them where they can take time away from the formal instructions (especially for younger children) at school, even at home my child had a few sensory toys a popper, coloured timer they could watch and a favourite books.
- Educate children about different emotions can they differentiate between happy, sad, surprised, excited, etc. A good way is to role play with your child and see if you can get them to react in different ways.
- Developing their emotional vocabulary. Children can become frustrated and withdrawn because they are unable to explain what it is they are feeling or they will feel overwhelmed and not be able to process the emotions. Teach children and young people the words they need to describe different emotions. Even as adults we find this hard, imagine how it is for a child.

- Creating consequences where the child or young person is rewarded for good behaviours and discouraged from unwanted behaviours. Children love gamification techniques, 'levelling up' this is always a good start for them to understand and grow.

Physical or Psychological Impairment

When a child has any physical or psychological impairment, they need plenty of assistance, and most of their weekly routine is dedicated to therapies. Yet, it is crucial that you allow your child some time for enjoying playtime. Some parents feel overwhelmed when looking after a disabled child, and playing with them is a great way of bonding: "It's important for you to play with your child often in order to improve your relationship and help him cope with his physical challenges" (Doheny, 2010).

According to Sara Doschadis, from Monroe Carell Jr. Children's Hospital at Vanderbilt in Nashville, any material can be adapted to make it suitable for a child's special needs (Doheny, 2010):

> For instance, a handle on a paintbrush can be extended to help a child with below-average hand coordination. A basketball hoop can be lowered to

> accommodate a child in a wheelchair. [...] Your child's physical or occupational therapist can help you with suggestions for play adaptation.

Give your child opportunities to role play, especially fantasy. When they dress up, put on makeup, and pretend to be their favourite characters, their imagination is sparked and they get to live all kinds of experiences, unlimited by their disability. Make sure you encourage children with crutches, a wheelchair, or an orthopaedic walker in all kinds of games, celebrations, and even dancing with them! Let them choose their costumes and don't try to hide their devices because they are nothing to be ashamed of. This way, they'll feel they can have fun with their peers not *despite* their disability but exactly the way they are.

Visually Impaired

"The famous blind Italian educator Augusto Romagnoli indicates that the blind child acquires through play the awareness of self, of the others and of their otherness, experiences solidarity and cooperation" (Tzvetkova-Arsova & Zappaterra, 2016). Children with visual impairment can enjoy sensory play as well as role-playing based on verbal skills and actions.

They usually have the same cognitive skills as children their same age, although sometimes the social stages of play get delayed because of the child's difficulties to imitate other children (Tzvetkova-Arsova & Zappaterra, 2016). The parent or educator can provide a great role model for teaching the child some skills through direct interaction, clear verbal instructions, as well as through creating a safe environment.

Provided that they are assisted, needless to say, visually impaired children enjoy outdoor play as any other child! Most children with this kind of disability will develop great verbal and musical skills. Playing games with words and music can help them boost their self-confidence and feel at ease.

It's beneficial for these children to get plenty of time to play with peers without visual disabilities (Tzvetkova-Arsova & Zappaterra, 2016):

> The interaction between the blind child and his or her peers is important not only for access to associative and cooperative play in view of his or her development and pleasure, but mostly to give them the opportunity to fully exercise one of their rights: in fact, participation in recreational, play, leisure, and sport activities, including those in the school system.

Speech Impaired and/or Deaf

Play, among others benefits, helps children develop language. If the child has a speech impairment or they can't hear, adults in charge should help them learn strategies to integrate with their peers and engage in all kinds of play.

Deaf children who attend a special class can communicate through sign language with their classmates and their teacher once they have learned it because it is just like any other language: It allows them to express anything, from talking about how they feel to role-playing or engaging in symbolic play.

However, in a mixed classroom, children who lack the normal verbal skills of their peers often struggle not to be isolated. The same happens in families when only one sibling has a hearing impairment, and the other children can listen. In any case, it's important that we adults become the link between the speech impaired or deaf child with their listening siblings or classmates (National Deaf Children's Society, 2020):

> By participating in your children's play, you can promote communication skills and deaf-awareness techniques to your hearing child. For example, you could get your deaf child's attention before speaking to them. Your hearing child will learn to do the same

thing by copying your behaviour. You could also encourage both children to use signs so they learn their meanings through play.

If the child uses a hearing aid or an implant, make sure they keep it on during play, and try to provide them with a calm environment when playing. Too much noise can interfere with the child's growing verbal skills. The same applies to children who have trouble either expressing themselves in their language or understanding spoken language, despite their hearing being normal.

Parents and educators should:

Pay attention and accept different strategies the child uses for communicating.

Use language that is understood when approaching the child, use direct phrases, avoid being ambiguous, and give instructions one at a time.

Promote games that teach phonemic awareness, such as teaching them nursery rhymes.

Use visual cues.

Praise the child for every effort, to build their self-confidence and encourage them to keep communicating.

Inclusive Classroom or Home Environment

All great teachers have a few simple strategies for classroom activities up their sleeves for any eventuality. They will encourage hands-on learning and find ways to engage children of all ages and all abilities. Some say ten-year-olds love active participation with small inclusive groups. Others find eleven-year-olds benefit from interactive smart boards. Many have discovered that twelve-year-olds thrive on being given choices when performing tasks, be it a game, a worksheet, or a partner activity. It really is about catering to the individual and spotting which activities work for the child, by trying out different activities and methods until the correct formula is identified.

Despite the laws favouring inclusion in most countries, it is up to us to change our perception and make the world an inclusive place that embraces everyone with their unique capacities. School is a great place to start (Elizondo, 2019):

> Teachers, school administrators, and counsellors have the potential to reshape some of these attitudes and behaviours by creating opportunities for students to learn that disability and diversity are natural and by giving them positive school and playtime experiences with classmates who learn and do things differently.

The best news is when teachers and families join forces to create inclusive classrooms, *every* child benefits, not only the child with extra needs. We all need to change our perspective, and accept that behind that negative social construct there is fear and a lack of knowledge. Events such as ability awareness days, and inclusive playtime can reshape the way other people approach disability, putting aside our prejudices and embracing everything we have in common. We can all play and learn together, as we all like having friends and have something special to share with the world. "We need to start teaching children to believe in themselves as their own unique person and that learning from those who are different from ourselves only makes us stronger and wiser" (Elizondo, 2019).

Instead of focusing only on teaching the child with a disability how to play with other children, educators need to teach every student how to accept and include the child in all of their play. And always, make sure you share this goal with the families. Sometimes, a child only reproduces prejudice and discrimination because this is what they see at home.

Remember: Having an inclusive classroom is a privilege! Every child benefits when the classroom or the family becomes an inclusive environment in which differences are not only tolerated but embraced and accepted as part of our individuality.

Chapter 9

Play Ideas for Children

In *Happy Children Play* there have been many play ideas for children of all ages and even for adults too. Let's look at some of our favourites, including independent, calm, sensory, construction, active, music, mindfulness and self-regulation play. Below is a list of ideas for activities that don't require a lot of preparation.

Sensory Play

Children need to experience different textures, thicknesses, crunchiness, and scents. Promoting this has a huge impact on sensory awareness.

Sand and water. Create an area where children can be messy: at the kitchen sink, at an outside mud kitchen or in a sand and water tray. Children can see which toys can float, sink, make a car wash and clean their toys.

Playdough and slime. You can attempt to handle these materials with objects such as cookie cutters, plastic forks, knives, wooden sticks, or rolling pins.

Tactile Experience. Using raw pasta, rice or other materials found around the home; set up a play tray with your children's toys and let them explore different materials like tin foil or baking paper.

Construction Play

Unlike board games, which are more appropriate for older kids, construction games are not about competing against each other, but about breaking the child's own limits.

Build the tallest tower. Or the longest car racetrack. Or the weirdest spaceship! Let the children build, destroy, and rebuild. Encourage them to explain what they are doing and why.

Design an all-new car with linking cubes. Given a set of open-ended toys, two children will create two new, different toys. Ten children will create ten, new different toys as well!

Rainbow Pebbles are a range of tactile early years STEAM construction toys that offer more possibilities when it comes to teaching your children about shapes, colours, and fine motor skills.

Role Play

Make-believe and fantasy are core to a child's early years and should be encouraged in a safe and nurturing environment.

Playing the role of caregiver or parent. Offer them some of your clothes, hats or bags, and when you really want to delight your child, entrust them to play with grown-up objects, such as a wallet, a purse, keys or an old mobile phone. Be careful with batteries and small parts!

Turning into an animal. Cover a coffee table with an old sheet, and tell your toddler it's a transformation machine and as they walk in, they turn into animals. Jumping like frogs, running on their fours like a dog, waving their arms as they fly is a great way for children to move their bodies.

Playing superheroes. This is a great role-play for engaging with other children, expressing their fears and finding the tools to face them, and physically exploring their gross motor skills: running really fast, climbing tall trees, expressing their courage, etc. However, always supervise this play, to make sure they are not taking risks nor getting into physical fights; some toddlers are not aware yet that their cape *doesn't* actually make them fly.

Playing house. When your child prepares a meal with their pretend food, pretends to run a supermarket, takes their dolls to the doctor, or transforms the armchair into a driver's seat, they are recreating everyday events, learning from these situations, and gaining a better understanding them.

Active Play

Children can be so expressive and inventive and yet might find it hard to tell the best stories. Enacting the narrative is a steppingstone to expressing their thoughts while developing coordination.

Floor is Lava, building dens, obstacle course and playing floor is lava around the living areas with my children.

Obstacle course build an an obstacle course with pillows and cushions, or a spider web with a ball of string if you are inside and have limited room or use the park, equipment.

Build a Den Your child can build a den with furniture and blankets inside ot in the woodlands with sticks, trees, branches and so much more.

Treasure map let's Explore nature make your own treasure map with things you have to find, either write a list of items or for younger children use colours as the

Music Play

The idea is not to get a perfect result but to explore where the sound comes from, and have a great time while learning.

Shadow Dancing Turn off the lights in the room and give the children torches. Make the light circles "dance" to the rhythm of the music.

Shadow puppets You just need a torch, your fingers, and a good imagination. Use your fingers to make shapes in the light. My children always loved this just before bed.

Make you own instrument Give your children the supplies they need to craft and decorate their own musical instruments, such as homemade shakers filled with beans, drums made from cans, or handmade string instruments with elastic bands.

Nursery rhymes are a great resource for developing phonemic awareness, something that later will help them develop reading and writing skills. You can show them pictures of the rhymes, repeat them, create some different tunes for them.

Mindfulness Play

Recognising your body's movements and thinking about their body without any prejudging is a fabulous skill to develop.

Yoga and Stretching. Ask your child to stretch their toes forwards and backward while sitting on the floor with their legs stretched. Then, tell them to bend over and reach for their toes. Either standing up or sitting comfortably, ask them to shrug their shoulders, first the left one, then the right one and so on.

Balance. Tell them to stand up and pretend they are walking along a tightrope. If they are old enough, they can do it on tiptoes.

Breathing. Imagine their belly is a balloon of their favourite colour. Breathe in and inflate the balloon. As they breathe out, tell them to imagine the air around them turning into that same colour.

Sensory Jars. Either make a sensory jar with them of their favourite things alternatively. Give them a glitter jar and ask them to shake it, then stare at it until everything settles.

Self Regulation Play

The way a child manages his or her emotions can be worked upon; children learn to review and regulate their feelings.

Red Light, Green Light. Children move on the green light and stop on the red light. Don't get caught moving on the red light. This is a great way for children to learn basic of self-regulation with no equipment or preparation.

Freeze Dance. This is an easy game to just turn on music have children walk, wriggle, dance, the quicker the beat the faster they go. When music stops children have to freeze. Great way for children to learn basic of self-regulation with no equipment or preparation.

Memory games. There is a great emoji game. You have to match an emoji that with a picture or even colour (e.g red is anger, blue is sad), showing how you feel if you see this. It maybe swimming in the sea picture, playing sport, a scary ghost a messy room, playing with friends.

Storytelling together. Develop a story together choose 3 items around the house that need to be in it. For. E.g. a banana, chair and pencils. Allow the child to start the story, then you add to it.

Conclusion

As you have read already, we really want to highlight the importance of play for babies, toddlers, children of all ages, teenagers and even adults. It is a way we develop our skills, have fun, and produce natural hormones to recharge the body.

Throughout this book, we have seen how children benefit from play in so many ways we can hardly count them. Play should be a child's main occupation, and they should engage in different kinds of play several times a day.

Here are some key take-aways from this book:

Play begins even before a child is born, and changes dramatically over the course of the first five years of life, to reflect both a child's development as well as their newly acquired social skills. No matter how young your child is, they should still be given plenty of opportunities to play.

Parten and Piaget both came up with theories about the stages of play. Although Piaget is considered the first one to think about children as entirely different from "little adults," Parten's social theory of play is more accurate when it comes to explaining how children progressively engage in social play.

Parents, caregivers, and educators are hugely important during a child's play. Notwithstanding the different parenting approaches, we can all learn how to play with our children, and we benefit from these interactions as well because they help us bond. However, children don't need us to play with them all the time! When it comes to spending time together, quality is more important than quantity.

Solitary play has a lot of benefits for children as well. While for some of them it comes naturally, others have a hard time and display clinginess. There are plenty of strategies we can implement for stimulating independent play in children.

Just as children need time for active play, they also need moments to calm down. Including quiet play ideas into their routine may help them release the tensions and learn better.

Play also offers important benefits when it comes to helping a child be emotionally ready for school. Whether by teaching them basic social skills or by helping them gain the necessary confidence for taking risks, play is crucial during this transition.

Role-play and structured play (such as board games) also contribute significantly to the child's implicit learning, but these kinds of play also allow us, adults, to learn about our children and give them tools to face challenging situations.

Children with special education needs, such as children with disabilities of any kind, may find, through play and the loving guidance of an adult, a way to connect with their peers in an inclusive environment that allows them to become a better version of themselves and embrace their differences instead of overlooking them.

There is more behind children's behaviour when they are showing signs of not being able to self-regulate. Let's look beyond the behaviour and at the 5 domains (Biological, emotional, cognitive, social & prosocial) and what could be the potential trigger areas. Try and identify, work and educate the child with coping mechanisms, make adaptions at home and in the classroom.

Children need to feel safe, supported and empowered by the caregivers around them. Try taking time out of your day to spend quality time with your children. Look at their interests, involve them with yours.

There are many ideas throughout this book of different play ideas, being inclusive, taking time out to spend time with your children. Creating memorable experiences, helping them develop into happy, healthy children.

Now that you have gained all this knowledge about the importance of play, and that you have new tools, you can start implementing them right away at home with your own family, or in the classroom. What are you waiting for? Not only will your children be the most fortunate, but you will benefit from being their play companion as well.

Happy children love to play and spending time with your child, bonding making quality connections will be their most memorable experiences. Let's develop happy, healthy children who will become life-long learners and leaders through play!

Glossary

Glossary

ADHD: Abbreviation used for attention deficit hyperactivity disorder.

Autism Spectrum Disorder ASD: It refers to any within a group of developmental disorders that affect social interaction, the ability to communicate, the presence of repetitive behaviours, or a restriction in interests.

Fine motor skills: The corporal abilities that involve a specific group of muscles in the hands and wrists. For example, using a fork, drawing, or piling up a tower of wooden blocks.

Free play: Activity in which children engage without following set rules or a time limit.

Gross motor skills: Physical abilities that control the muscles for movements such as walking, running, swimming, or kicking a ball.

Lovey: Also known as "comfort object" or "transitional object," it's a toy (or any safe item) that helps babies get over separation anxiety by providing them security and reassurance.

Messy play: Another expression for "sensory play," which means, the free, open-ended exploration of different materials that stimulate the use of the five senses.

Mindfulness: A practice that focuses on maintaining a state of complete awareness of our emotions, thoughts, and experiences, without judging them.

Object permanence: The understanding that an object still exists even if it's not currently visible.

Self Regulation: The ability to understand and manage your behaviour and your reactions to feelings and things happening around you.

STEM or STEAM toys: The acronym for science, technology, engineering, mathematics, and sometimes also art. The term is used for describing toys that promote learning abilities in those areas.

Structured play: Activity in which, unlike in free play, children have an established goal. It can be competitive or cooperative.

References

Albrecht, K. (2016, August). *Understanding and encouraging toddler play*. Community Playthings. https://www.communityplaythings.co.uk/learning-library/articles/whats-play-got-to-do-with-it

Anderson-McNamee, J. & Bailey, S. (2010, April). "The importance of play in early childhood development" in *MontGuide* (MT201003HR New 4/10). Montana State University. Retrieved from: https://www.tulsaeducare.org/wp-content/uploads/2012/01/Educare-Content-G-Articles-Importance-of-Play-Article.pdf

Arora, M. (2022, January 1). *Solitary (independent) play–Benefits and why it is good for kids*. Firstcry. https://parenting.firstcry.com/articles/solitary-independent-play-benefits-and-tips-to-encourage-it-in-a-child/

Bradley, S. (2021, May 16). *Everything you need for your baby: 3–6 months*. VeryWell Family. https://www.verywellfamily.com/everything-you-need-for-your-baby-3-to-6-months-4845886

Brody, B. (2021, February 25). *What are the different parenting styles?* WebMD. https://www.webmd.com/parenting/features/parenting-styles

Chua, A. (2011). *Battle hymn of the tiger mother*. Penguin Books.

Cleveland Clinic. (2020, August 13). *10 tips for dealing with sibling rivalry*. https://health.clevelandclinic.org/sibling-rivalry-tips-5-for-prevention-5-for-intervention/

Cummings, W. R. (2020, January 4). *Emotional dysregulation in children and teens*. PsychCentral. https://psychcentral.com/blog/childhood-behavioral/2020/01/emotional-dysregulation-in-children-and-teens#1

Davidson, S. (2017, March 21). *Top 6 benefits of board games for kids.* Medium. https://medium.com/@ShawnDavison1/top-6-benefits-of-board-games-for-kids-111db7659ba7

DeJeu, E. (2022, June 22). *Baby lovey–How and when to introduce (and what should the lovey be, anyway?).* The Baby Sleep Site. https://www.babysleepsite.com/sleep-training/baby-lovey-how-when-why/

Dean, J. (2021a). *Piaget stages of development theory.* PsyBlog. https://www.spring.org.uk/2021/08/piaget-stages-of-development.php

Dean, J. (2021b). *Types of play: 6 stages important for your child's development.* PsyBlog. https://www.spring.org.uk/2021/05/types-of-play.php

Doheny, K. (2010, October 14). *Playtime for children with physical disabilities.* WebMD. https://www.webmd.com/children/features/playtime-physical-disabilities

Early Childhood Education in Ethiopia. (2022, February 20). *Why play matters most in early education programs.* Early Childhood Education in Ethiopia. https://www.earlyeducationethiopia.org/why-play-matters-most-in-early-education-programs/

Early Years Matters. (2021). *Play and learning.* Early Years Matters. https://www.earlyyearsmatters.co.uk/eyfs/a-unique-child/play-learning/

Elizondo, M. (2019, May 7). *Comfort conversations: The importance of positive playtime & learning experiences for kids of all abilities*. Wheel-Life. https://wheel-life.com/comfort-conversations-importance-positive-playtime-learning-experiences-kids-abilities/

Encyclopaedia Britannica (2022, September 12). *Jean Piaget*. https://www.britannica.com/biography/Jean-Piaget

Ewing, R. (2020, July 22). *Structured play vs. free play*. Bricks 4 Kidz. https://www.bricks4kidz.com/blog/structured-play-vs-free-play/

Faure, M. (2021, February 6). *How playing helps develop emotional regulation in children*. Play Sense. https://playsense.org/playing-developing-emotional-regulation-in-children/

Glembocki, V. (2012, October 7). *Learning to play with your kids*. Parents. https://www.parents.com/parenting/better-parenting/advice/learning-to-play-with-kids/

Hargraves, V. (2022, February 1). *What is digital play?* https://theeducationhub.org.nz/what-is-digital-play/

Huleatt, H. (2018, June). *role-play—Making sense of the world*. Community Playthings. https://www.communityplaythings.co.uk/learning-library/articles/role-play-making-sense-of-the-world

Ireland, A. (2015). *Child anxiety: What to do if your child is anxious, worried or upset*. A Lust for Life. https://www.alustforlife.com/tools/mental-health/child-anxiety-what-to-do-if-your-child-is-anxious-worried-or-upset

Kensington, J. (2019). *Homeschooling vs. traditional schooling*. Get Homeschooled. https://gethomeschooled.com/homeschooling-vs-traditional-schooling/

Lepucki, E. (2021, June 15). *Don't play with your kids. Seriously*. The New York Times Magazine. https://www.nytimes.com/2021/06/15/magazine/kids-play.html

Li, P. (2022, October 6). *Importance of play in early childhood (9 benefits & infographic)*. Parenting for Brain. https://www.parentingforbrain.com/benefits-play-learning-activities-early-childhood/

Li, P. (2022, October 2). *Parten's 6 social stages of play and why they are important*. Parenting for Brain. https://www.parentingforbrain.com/stages-of-play/

The Little Dreamers Nursery. (2022, June 30). *5 important benefits of role-play in early childhood.* https://dreamersnursery.com/benefits-of-role-play-in-early-childhood/

McIlroy, T. (2021). *22 simple calming activities for kids*. Empowered Parents. https://empoweredparents.co/calming-activities-for-kids/

Merali, S. and Orson, K. (2016, August 15). *15 playful ways to solve sibling rivalry*. Hand in Hand. https://www.handinhandparenting.org/2016/08/15-playful-ways-handle-sibling-rivalry/

Merriam-Webster Dictionary (2019). https://www.merriam-webster.com/dictionary

Mlynek, A. (2020, October 30). *An age-by-age guide to playing with your kid*. Today's Parent. https://www.todaysparent.com/family/family-life/how-to-play-with-your-kid/

Mundy, S. (2021, April 9). *Returning to school: How to support children's emotional well-being through play*. EDXEducation. https://edxeducation.com/returning-to-school-how-to-support-childrens-emotional-well-being-through-play/

National Childbirth Trust. (2019) *Screen time for babies and toddlers: the evidence*. NCT. https://www.nct.org.uk/baby-toddler/games-and-play/screen-time-for-babies-and-toddlers-evidence

National Deaf Children's Society. (2020, June 15). *How to support your deaf child playing with their hearing siblings*. https://www.ndcs.org.uk/blog/how-to-support-your-deaf-child-playing-with-their-hearing-siblings/

NSN Group of Schools (2022, April 8). *Best activities for a shy child*. https://www.nsnschools.com/best-activities-for-a-shy-child/

Raising Children Network (2019). *Outdoor play*. https://raisingchildren.net.au/toddlers/play-learning/outdoor-play/outdoor-play

Ranson, A. (2014, May 14). *10 calming activities for wind down time*. The Imagination Tree. https://theimaginationtree.com/10-calm-down-activities-for-kids/

Reed, K. (2022, April 4). What is messy play and why is it important? *It's a Mother Thing*. https://www.amotherthing.com/what-the-heck-is-messy-play-and-why-is-it-important/

Rock, A. (2022, September 14). *When do kids start preschool?* VeryWell Family. https://www.verywellfamily.com/is-your-child-ready-to-start-preschool-2764924

Rudy, L. (2022, May 15). *The reasons autistic children play differently*. VeryWell Health. https://www.verywellhealth.com/autistic-child-form-of-play-259884

Rymanowicz, K. (2015, October 6). *The power of play–Part 1: Stages of play*. Michigan State University. https://www.canr.msu.edu/news/the_power_of_play_part_1_stages_of_play

Sears, W. & Sears, M. (2001). *The attachment parenting book: A commonsense guide to understanding and nurturing your baby*. Little, Brown Spark.

Shakibaie, S. (2021) *7 fun games to improve emotional regulation*. Ready Kids. https://readykids.com.au/7-fun-games-to-improve-emotional-regulation/

Skenazi, L. (2010). *Free-range kids: How to raise safe, self-reliant children (without going nuts with worry)*. Jossey-Bass.

Stewart, D. H. (2022). *Kindergarten readiness: Is your child ready for school?* Babycenter. https://www.babycenter.com/child/learning-and-education/kindergarten-readiness-is-your-child-ready-for-school_67232

Strauss, E. (2021, July 5). *What happens to you when you play with your kids*. CNN. https://edition.cnn.com/2021/07/05/health/play-with-your-kids-health-benefits-wellness/index.html

Taylor-Klauss, E. (2022). *How to help your kid become a good sport.* Impact Parents. https://impactparents.com/blog/complex-kids/how-to-help-your-kid-become-a-good-sport/

Toth, W. (2014, December 6). *Teaching kids how to be good sports.* Parents. https://www.parents.com/kids/development/behavioral/teaching-kids-how-to-be-good-sports/

Tzvetkova-Arsova, M. & Zappaterra, T. (2016, January). *Play in children with visual impairments*. ResearchGate. https://www.researchgate.net/publication/316306585_Play_in_Children_with_Visual_Impairments

UNICEF. (2019). *The Convention on the Rights of the Child: The children's version*. UNICEF. https://www.unicef.org/child-rights-convention/convention-text-childrens-version

Vivvi.™. (2021, June 3). *Benefits of roleplay for kids: It's more than just make believe*. https://vivvi.com/blog/articles/roleplay-for-kids-benefits

WebMD Editorial Contributors. (2000). *What's it like in the womb?* WebMD. https://www.webmd.com/baby/features/in-the-womb

Wolfe, K. (2020, January 14). *How to help a clingy child play independently*. Hand in Hand. https://www.handinhandparenting.org/2020/01/help-clingy-child-play-independently/

Index

Thank you to James, William, Edward

& to my own parents, siblings

for inspiring and supporting me

in writing this book, *Happy Children Play*.

Printed in Poland
by Amazon Fulfillment
Poland Sp. z o.o., Wrocław

35308281R00101